# The Most Incredible FREE Gift Ever

## ($573.94 Worth of Pure Money-Making Information)

Dan Kennedy & Bill Glazer are offering an incredible opportunity for you to see WHY Glazer-Kennedy Insider's Circle™ is known as "THE PLACE" where entrepreneurs seeking FAST and Dramatic Growth and greater Control, Independence, and Security come together. Dan & Bill want to give you **$573.94 worth of pure Money-Making Information** including a FREE month as an 'Elite' Gold Member of Glazer-Kennedy's Insider's Circle™. You'll receive a steady stream of MILLIONAIRE Maker Information including:

## * Glazer-Kennedy University: Series of 3 Webinars (Value = $387.00)

### The 10 "BIG Breakthroughs in Business Life with Dan Kennedy
- HOW Any Entrepreneur or Sales Professional can Multiply INCOME by 10X
- **HOW to Avoid Once and For All being an "Advertising Victim"**
- The "Hidden Goldmine" in Everyone's Business and HOW to Capitalize on it
- **The BIGGEST MISTAKE most Entrepreneurs make in their Marketing**
- And the BIGGEEE...Getting Customers Seeking You Out.

### The ESSENTIALS to Writing Million Dollar Ads & Sales Letters BOTH Online & Offline with Marketing & Advertising Coach, Bill Glazer
- How to INCREASE the Selling Power of All Your Advertising by Learning the 13 "Must Have" Direct Response Principles
- **Key Elements that Determine the Success of Your Website**
- HOW to Craft a Headline the Grabs the Reader's Attention
- **How to Create an Irresistible Offer that Melts Away Any Resistance to Buy**
- The Best Ways to Create Urgency and Inspire IMMEDIATE Response
- **"Insider Strategies" to INCREASE Response that you Must be using both ONLINE & Offline**

### The ESSENTIALS of Productivity & Implementation for Entrepreneurs w/ Peak Performance Coach Lee Milteer
- How to Almost INSTANTLY be MORE Effective, Creative, Profitable, and Take MORE Time Off
- **HOW to Master the "Inner Game" of Personal Peak Productivity**
- How to Get MORE Done in Less Time
- **HOW to Get Others to Work On Your Schedule**
- How to Create Clear Goals for SUCCESSFUL Implementation
- And Finally the BIGGEE...How to Stop Talking and Planning Your Dreams and Start Implementing Them into Reality

## * 'Elite' Gold Insider's Circle Membership (One Month Value = $59.97):

- ### An Issue of *The No B.S.® Marketing Letter:*

  Each issue is at least 20 pages – usually MORE – Overflowing with **the latest Marketing & MoneyMaking Strategies**. Current members refer to it as a day-long intense seminar in print, arriving by first class mail every month. There are ALWAYS terrific examples of **"What's-Working-NOW"** **Strategies,** timely Marketing news, trends, ongoing teaching of Dan Kennedy's Most IMPORTANT Strategies… and MORE. As soon as it arrives in your mailbox you'll want to find a quiet place, grab a highlighter, and devour every word.

- CD of an **EXCLUSIVE GOLD AUDIO INTERVIEW:**

These are EXCLUSIVE interviews with <u>successful users of direct response advertising, leading experts and entrepreneurs in direct marketing, and famous business authors and speakers</u>. Use them to turn commuting hours into "POWER Thinking" hours.

### * The New Member No B.S.® Income Explosion Guide & CD (Value = $29.97)

This resource is <u>especially designed for NEW MEMBERS</u> to show them HOW they can join the thousands of Established Members **creating exciting sales and PROFIT growth** in their Business, Practices, or Sales Careers & Greater SUCCESS in their Business lives.

### Income Explosion FAST START Tele-Seminar with Dan Kennedy, Bill Glazer, and Lee Milteer (Value = $97.00)

Attend from the privacy and comfort of your home or office…hear a DYNAMIC discussion <u>of Key Advertising, Marketing, Promotion, Entrepreneurial & Phenomenon strategies</u>, PLUS answers to the most Frequently Asked Questions about these Strategies

## * You'll also get these Exclusive "Members Only" Perks:

- **Special FREE Gold Member CALL-IN TIMES:** Several times a year, Dan & I schedule Gold-Member ONLY Call-In times
- **Gold Member RESTRICTED ACCESS WEBSITE:** Past issues of the *No B.S.® Marketing Letter*, articles, special news, etc.
- **Continually Updated MILLION DOLLAR RESOURCE DIRECTORY** with Contacts and Resources Dan & his clients use.

To activate your MOST INCREDIBLE FREE GIFT EVER you only pay a one-time charge of $19.95 (or $29.95 for Int'l subscribers) to cover postage (this is for everything). **After your 1-Month FREE test-drive, you will automatically continue at the <u>lowest</u> Gold Member price of $59.97 per month. Should you decide to cancel your membership, you can do so at any time by calling Glazer-Kennedy Insider's Circle™ at 410-825-8600 or faxing a cancellation note to 410-825-3301 (Monday through Friday 9am – 5pm). Remember, your credit card will NOT be charged the low monthly membership fee until the beginning of the next month, which means you will receive 1 full issue to read, test, and profit from all of the powerful techniques and strategies you get from being an Insider's Circle Gold Member. And of course, it's impossible for you to lose, because if you don't absolutely LOVE everything you get, you can simply cancel your membership before next month and never get billed a single penny for membership.**

---

**\*EMAIL REQUIRED IN ORDER TO NOTIFY YOU ABOUT THE GLAZER-KENNEDY UNIVERSITY WEBINARS AND FAST START TELESEMINAR\***

Name _____ Business Name _____

Address _____

City _____ State _____ Postal Code _____ Country _____

e-mail* _____

Phone _____ Fax _____

**Credit Card Instructions to Cover $19.95 ($29.95 Int'l) for Shipping & Handling:**

____Visa ____MasterCard ____ American Express ____ Discover

Credit Card Number _____ Exp. Date _____

Signature _____ Date _____

**FAX BACK TO 410-825-3301**
**Or Go To: www.freegiftfrom.com/kessler**
**Or mail to: 401 Jefferson Ave, Towson, MD 21286**

How One of America's Legendary Rogues
Marketed "The Goat Testicles Solution"
and Made Millions

# MAKING THEM
# BELIEVE

## The 21 PRINCIPLES and LOST SECRETS
## of DR. J.R. BRINKLEY-STYLE MARKETING

# DAN S. KENNEDY
## AND CHIP KESSLER

Glazer-Kennedy
publishing

*An Imprint of Morgan James Publishing*

# MAKING THEM
# BeLieve

Copyright © 2010 Dan Kennedy and Chip Kessler

ISBN: 978-0-98237-938-7 (Paperback)
Library of Congress Control Number: 2010922103

Published by:

GLAZER-KENNEDY PUBLISHING
*An Imprint of Morgan James Publishing*

1225 Franklin Ave Ste 32, Garden City, NY 11530-1693
Toll Free 800-485-4943
www.MorganJamesPublishing.com

Cover/Interior Design by:
Rachel Lopez
rachel@r2cdesign.com

In an effort to support local communities, raise awareness and funds, Morgan James Publishing donates one percent of all book sales for the life of each book to Habitat for Humanity. Get involved today, visit **www.HelpHabitatForHumanity.org.**

# The Readers

"This is one killer book! I read it from cover to cover, non-stop, annoying all in my home. I couldn't put it down. It reads like a Grisham novel but lays out a 21-step blueprint for business success. My warning to readers: after consuming, if you fail to get a `marketing erection' (enormous inspiration), seek professional help immediately!"

## —JERRY JONES

One of the leading dental practice marketers in America. Jerry has delivered tens of thousands of patients to dental practices year after year, with his innovative advertising, direct-mail and marketing campaigns. ButtslnOps.com. JerryJonesDirect.com

"...captured and held my Interest from first to last page. Getting an In-depth look at the marketing gambits of 'the amazing Dr. Brinkley' is fascinating enough, but the dissection and analysis provided by Dan Kennedy and Chip Kessler is fascinating and valuable!"

## —DR. CHRIS TOMSHACK

CEO, HealthSource Chiropractic, the world's largest franchise organization in the chiropractic profession. HealthSource has been recognized by Entrepreneur Magazine as the leading franchise organization in the health services category for two consecutive years. HenithSourceChiro.com. HealthSourceSuccess.com

"Dan Kennedy and Chip Kessler do a brilliant job presenting one of American history's most interesting, imaginative entrepreneurs, Dr. John Brinkley.  Whether you find Dr. Brinkley charming or villainous, you have to be in awe of his outrageous marketing antics - and you will find countless marketing ideas In his work useful for any business."

## —DR. GREG NIELSEN D.C.

Dr. Nielsen had the good fortune of finding Dan Kennedy 25 years ago when first graduated from chiropractic college—and he has never looked back!  Doc's own exceptionally effective and unusual marketing is frequently featured in Dan's newsletters and books. wwwDocNielsenList.com

# table & contents

# introduction

## IF YOUR ERECTION LASTS LONGER THAN FOUR HOURS...

*By Dan S. Kennedy*

As I write this page, I am a few weeks into my 35th year breathing, eating, sleeping and earning my living with advertising, marketing and promotion—in many ways, making hay from hype. I am not at all ashamed of that truth. I love my work. So I am a great fan of outrageous, over the top advertising and marketing, all the way to flim-flammery.

One of my favorites, as I write this, is the widely run, extremely successful campaign for "Amish heaters"—actually ordinary space heaters designed to look like fireplaces, stuck inside rolling wood boxes with mantles, those; (only) the wood boxes manufactured by "Amish craftsmen" and then sold at premium—or if you prefer, inflated—prices via copy-rich, story-rich full-page newspaper ads, magazine ads, direct-mail pieces and even a TV infomercial. Ironic, since the Amish can't even have these things in their own homes or see the infomercial selling them. Amusing, because the Amish have nothing whatsoever to do with the 'furnace', only its wood frame. But a benign, pretty much harmless flim-flam. The ad is a masterpiece, and I admire it like I imagine a connoisseur of art admires a great painting hung in a museum.

Another favorite, contemporary flim-flam is the now ten year old, still daring presentation by the Subway® chain of eating gigantic, foot-long loaves of bread as a path to weight loss. Another is Starbucks' calling its small coffee a "Grande."

Anyway, that gives you a bit of insight into my twisted mind. I have studied the lives and, to the greatest extent possible the marketing and promotion strategies of great flim-flam artists like Barnum and Houdini, and this book owes some debt of inspiration to a book about Barnum's marketing by a friend of mine, Joe Vitale: *There's A Customer Born Every Minute*. Modern-day Barnums fascinate too, like Trump. But the most audacious from past centuries fascinate most, as they had to pull off their grandiose schemes and escapades without the array of media and ready access to it that we have today. One can only imagine the havoc this book's subject, the rascally Dr. Brinkley might have wrought, had he had the Internet, e-mail, Twitter, YouTube and TV infomercials to work with.

When I first found and read Pope Brock's brilliantly written book *Charlatan*, about Dr. John Brinkley, I couldn't wait to get copies into the hands of my friends in the marketing world, and to recommend it in my newsletters. Dr. Brinkley was in the erectile dysfunction treatment business before blue pills or TV commercials, instead selling surgical grafting of goat testicles to men in need. Yes, you read that right. Then when I discovered that within the Glazer-Kennedy Insider's Circle™ Membership*, we had the husband of a direct descendant of John Brinkley, himself an able marketer and passionate student of the game, and in possession of insider knowledge about Brinkley, and with access to a vast archive of Brinkley ads, pamphlets, sales letters, radio broadcasts and the like, I was kid at entry to candy store eager to explore. That led to this book, to which I've happily contributed—although, frankly, my co-author Chip Kessler, husband of a cousin of the less-than-esteemed Dr. Brinkley, did the lion's share of the work. In addition to this book, Chip and I have also collaborated on a much more in-depth Course on Brinkley marketing strategies, introduced at the end of this book.

In essence, the book *Charlatan* tells the John Brinkley story, and if you haven't read it, you should, as companion to this. Our book delves deeply into how he did what he did; the psychology behind the marketing and promotion that made Dr. Brinkley a national sensation.

Beyond being entertaining and of prurient interest to anyone with twisted mind like mine, anyone who thinks that Jerry Della Femina was right when he said that advertising is the most fun you can have with your clothes on, this book does serve practical, profitable purpose. Honest.

Every proposition that Dr. John Brinkley sold and promoted and popularized—as well as his own presentation of himself as a trustworthy man of medicine—was preposterous, outrageous, and incredible. No one of sound mind should have been gulled, but tens of thousands of consumers, media, and even others in the medical community were. It has long been my contention that what successfully sells the *in*credible can be used even more effectively to sell the credible.

In this book, Chip and I have painstakingly dissected—pardon the use of that term—the ideas, strategies, tactics that Brinkley used and converted them to principles you can use to promote yourself and your business much more persuasively than ever before.

Dr. Brinkley was also a pioneer of media. One of the first, if not the first, to use radio as a direct-response media, even a unique form of infomercial on radio. Given that we operate in a brave new world of proliferating new media, there's much to be learned from the thinking of a man who was ten steps ahead of the rest of the world in using all that was available in his time.

If nothing else, this book may embolden you and motivate you to push your own envelope a bit farther and be more creative and aggressive, even have more fun, making yourself and your business famous. And please do. We have more than enough "ordinary" in every category.

I hope you enjoy the book, and as always, personally welcome your comments at my direct fax line: 602-269-3113.

*Dan S. Kennedy*

# foreword #1

*by James Brinkley*

> James Brinkley is a cousin of Dr. Brinkley's. He has
> been in various business enterprises throughout his life.

I'm a firm believer in genes playing an important role in what people end up doing in life, whether it's a career in business, sports, or the arts. I think that it just happens to be in the "Brinkley genes," when it comes to a great many Brinkley's, that we wind up as businessmen and entrepreneurs. This was how it was growing up in my parent's household with my brothers, including my niece Debbie's father William Hoy Junior, and my sister. My parents were both businesspeople and their example was there for all of us kids to see at an early age.

I remember as a child I used to dream about doing certain things later in life and they were all pretty much business related. For instance as a teenager, I dreamed about getting a motel and it gave me a real warm feeling; the excitement of owning something like that. I've just always had an interest in business. It's what led me to start selling newspapers on the street when I was only eight or nine years old just to get some extra spending money. I'd get eight newspapers a day and it would take me about four or five hours walking all over town to sell those eight papers. I'd made two and a half cents for each one I sold. It laid the foundation for my business career that lasts through today including my latest project: housing developments outside of Jacksonville, Florida.

I know in my case, for example, that whenever I go to a strange city I'll look for Brinkley's in the telephone book, and so many times they are involved in running businesses. So it just seems to me that there's a gene that leads many a Brinkley into becoming an entrepreneur.

To be in business and to be an entrepreneur, you have to be a bit of a risk taker. Of course sometimes becoming a risk taker, whether it's in your business life or your personal life comes out of necessity. I've speculated about this quite a bit myself, and it seems to me as if a great many entrepreneurs are more interested in learning as much as they can about their business, than the everyday book style learning we received in school.

My brother Walt was a good example of this. He didn't have much of an education, maybe just as far as the second or third grade, whatever it was. And yet he went on to become a millionaire. He had the ambition to make something of himself and to have something, so he became an entrepreneur out of necessity. Walt began right after World War II, owning a restaurant that my father built for him and later had our Dad put an addition on to the building to sell coal. An interesting note here, and a testimony to Walt's business instincts, was that when our father had built the restaurant building for Walt, he put a provision into the lease that stated Walt couldn't sell beer. But when Walt asked him to put on the addition to the restaurant in order to sell coal, there wasn't a provision in the additional lease that said anything about selling beer out of the new space. Walt began offering package beer and bringing in $500 to $600 dollars a week, which back then, was quite a bit of money. He was making that much just off the beer sales, not to mention what he was bringing in from the restaurant and his coal business. Later he bought some land himself and built some buildings and rented those out. Eventually, Walt ended up getting one of the first liquor licenses in our hometown of Johnson City, Tennessee. While I can't say that every Brinkley goes into business for him or herself, the ones who do seem to do very well for themselves.

What follows in this book are the marketing and business stories of two other Brinkley's that ventured out into the world and made names for themselves. One is our erstwhile cousin Dr. John R. Brinkley and the other is my great-grandfather Samuel Griffith Brinkley. Each, as in keeping with the Brinkley nature, had something special to offer, though both had very different kinds of items to market to the public.

I never got to meet either man, though in the case of my grandfather, my mother would tell us how he was an excellent singer and that he also liked to preach some. She said he was great at being able to throw his voice, or what in later year's people did professionally and were called ventriloquists. Then of course there was his most important and unusual characteristic, which you'll learn more about, later in this book.

As for Dr. John R. Brinkley, I really didn't know much about his exploits until I read the book *Charlatan*. I'll say this; I'm not ashamed of him. In fact, I kind of admire the fact that he was that capable of getting his message out, even though he was a rogue. You can't deny that he had the intelligence and the ingenuity to be able to do the things that he did, and do them successfully. If you're like me, you can't help but admire this man.

For me, whether it's a J.R. Brinkley or anyone that achieves a great deal of success in life, there are things that you can pinpoint, study, and learn from them. In Dr. Brinkley's case, his achievements were not the most ethical, but the marketing principals he employed have certainly stood the test of time.

It is my hope that you will take this spirit of discovery along with you as you go forward into the following pages.

SINCERELY,
*James Brinkley*
Orange Park, FL

# foreword #2

*by Deborah Brinkley Kessler*

> *Deborah Brinkley Kessler is a cousin of*
> *Dr. John Brinkley's. "Growing up Brinkley" gave her*
> *special insight into the John Brinkley legacy.*

I never knew my father. His name was William Hoy Brinkley, Jr., and he was tragically killed in a work-related accident a few months before I was born.

Yet from an early age, I came to realize that being a member of the Brinkley family meant I was part of a unique clan. First and foremost was their uncanny ability to handle money. I've often joked that being a Brinkley meant knowing and respecting the value of a dollar. Perhaps that's why I received my college degree in accounting and have practiced the trade for a number of years.

While I chose to keep track of money in a nuts and bolts sense, a great many of the immediate members of my Brinkley family chose a path that allowed them to earn it as businessmen and entrepreneurs. My grandparents ran a local hotel and also a restaurant; one of their sons (my

Uncle Walter) established the first liquor store in our town and other relatives were associated with one business or another. My last surviving uncle James Brinkley presently owns a couple of businesses in Florida.

In this book, you'll read about a couple of other Brinkley relatives. One is my great- great-grandfather Samuel Griffith Brinkley. He was destined to become one of the most memorable entertainers of his era. How his achieved this distinction is something I hope you enjoy learning about. Next is the main subject of these pages, one John R. Brinkley, a cousin from many years back.

While his various activities were of a questionable nature, one thing is certain; John R. Brinkley knew what he wanted out of life and devised ingenious methods to gain them. While I'm not a marketer, I am a consumer and for sheer nerve and an unwavering sense of style, you have to hand it to the man. According to my husband, Chip; who is an enthusiastic student of marketing under the leadership of his fellow author Dan Kennedy, John R. Brinkley was at the top of his game. Chip tells me that the beauty of John's marketing is how far ahead of his time he was, and for sheer, unmitigated gall and daring, unmatched! That's the reason he and Mr. Kennedy were excited to tell you the story of John R. Brinkley, the marketer.

I, of course, heard 'the legend of Dr. Brinkley' from my family, but discovered much I didn't know when reading Pope Brock's book about his life, *Charlatan*. Now I've learned much more about how John Brinkley did what he did from the research Chip and Mr. Kennedy have done in writing this book—sort of a manual of rogue marketing. I'm biased, but I'm sure you'll find it fascinating!

WITH BEST WISHES,
*Deborah Brinkley Kessler*
Johnson City, TN

# preface

*By Chip Kessler*

Perhaps it has something to do with the name ... Brinkley. They say you can't tell a book by its cover however when it comes to the Brinkley name one has to wonder. Has there ever been a clan so well versed in the art of marketing?

What follows are examples of how to do it "The Brinkley Way." Our main focus will be on one Dr. John R. Brinkley. Maybe you have heard of the good doctor courtesy of the book *Charlatan* (Three Rivers Press) published a few years back. In it, author Pope Brock takes us through the exploits of the world-renowned goat-gland physician. And if you're not yet up to speed on Dr. Brinkley and his exploits with goats and the human male body, you'll want to read *Charlatan* because it is a wild tale of an unabashed, consummate promoter.

Indeed there is much for all to learn from John R. Brinkley, both in these pages and in *Charlatan*. The latter is much more than the story of this North Carolina native, born in humble surroundings, advancing his career and becoming for a period of time one of the wealthiest physicians and surgeons in the world. Brock details how Brinkley became so well known that he ran for the office of Governor in the state of Kansas, where he'd gone on the achieve some of his greatest business success.

Our goal here is to present Dr. John Brinkley for what he really was, a master marketer and promoter. We will take a closer examination of the marketing strategies Brinkley employed, many of them revolutionary, for the period of the first half of the 20th century. As you'll discover, Brinkley was very savvy in the way he marketed his services, positioning himself and his medical techniques as "the answer."

Dr. Brinkley's remarkable success was based on a very simple equation: Problem/Agitate Problem/ Offer Solution; a formula my co-author, Dan Kennedy, has been teaching throughout his 35 years in the marketing field. Dr. John R. Brinkley identified a problem no one spoke about, dared to bring it into the open and talk about it, and played heavily on its emotional aspects in order to sell his solution—a radical one. Many years later, Pfizer followed Dr. Brinkley's blueprint to a 'T' in introducing and popularizing the less radical, modern solution for the same problem: Viagra®. Of course, all they've had to do is promote the taking of a little blue pill. The sheer genius of Dr. Brinkley is revealed by the degree of difficulty inherent in his marketing challenge: he was successfully able to guide his patients to: (1.) Parting with a great deal of money to gain the answer, and (2.) Going under the surgeon's knife.

Think about these two points for a moment.

No matter if you don't yet know exactly what Dr. Brinkley's intention was surgically speaking, nor what the exact extent of his Problem/

Solution axiom was: he was able to get men to willingly and gladly get cut open! How many physicians, especially back in Brinkley's time before the popularity of whole-hog plastic surgery that we have in the marketplace today, could claim to have such power over prospective patients? The answer was very few. Surely on this fact alone, any student of marketing would want to learn more about the doctor's strategies and tricks of the trade. Anyone engaged in promotion of self as expert, authority or celebrity, and anyone engaged in the promotion of a product or service that cures some ill, and anyone engaged in professional practice of any kind has to marvel at Dr. Brinkley's marketing of a radical, unheard of, frightening surgical solution.

I will leave you for now to ponder the marketing expertise of Dr. John R. Brinkley, in order to return to our original premise … that name, "Brinkley," and how it seems to lend itself to entrepreneurial excess. Elsewhere in this book you will read of another Brinkley, Samuel Griffith Brinkley. Sam Brinkley went on to become one of the most memorable characters of his time. I'll let you seek out his picture elsewhere in this book. I only wish I was right by your side to see the expression on your face when you come upon ol' Samuel. He was a living testament to letting your most unique asset make you a success. I hope that you enjoy reading about this gentleman, not only to learn his story but how he made a cottage industry of himself through his marketing expertise.

The Brinkley family's roots lie for the most part in the hills of Western North Carolina. To this day one can venture on a scenic highway that travels from the state line of Northeast Tennessee into the Tar Heel state and see the Brinkley presence. Just a few miles into North Carolina is the town of Elk Park. Here you will spot Brinkley Hardware just off the main highway. Inside is a vast selection of everything for the do-it-yourselfer or at least the man or woman that likes to think they are capable of such chores. A few miles further down the road, in the town of Newland is the Brinkley Motor Company. One can go on the lot and take his or her pick of the latest pre-owned automobiles. Both businesses have been staples of their respective towns dating all the way back to the time of Dr. John R. Brinkley. Back across the state line in Tennessee, the portion of the Brinkley family that settled in the town of Johnson City has been known for years for their business savvy. The list of Brinkley-owned entrepreneurial enterprises run the gamut of everything from hotels to restaurants to insurance sales to the town's first liquor store.

At this point, let us move forward. While being a successful television newscaster, entertainer, model/actress and writer is all fine and good, our intention here is to learn some of the finer points of marketing and how one man Dr. John R. Brinkley literally and figuratively took the nation by storm. How many people can make such a claim? His blueprint is available to see, and was available for us to assemble and comment on in this book, because Dr. Brinkley went about his business and his marketing in a larger-than-life-very-public- fashion. This statement in itself is one of the secrets to his success.

Here's a quick overview of his Marketing Principles we'll be looking at and illustrating in this book. It's quite possible some, many or even all of them are already familiar to you, but if so, it's the bold, brilliant execution of them that is worthy of your study and may inspire you to do more, go farther, push to greater extremes what you know, in promotion of yourself or your business. After all, knowledge is one thing; implementation, another.

➢ **List a problem** (already brought up but so vitally important as a starting point to effective marketing that it is well worth mentioning again plus one other note of interest here … the more gut-wrenching, earth-shattering, lay-awake-at-night and worry problem you can tap into the better)

➢ **Present a solution** (preferably one that captures the imagination)

➢ **Offer up yourself as the solution/savior** (a worthy goal for anyone that wishes to attract a large and loyal following of customers/clients/patients, etc.)

➢ **Tap into a well-defined niche** (as Dan Kennedy has pointed out in the past "there are riches in niches" and the more targeted your audience the better you're able to specifically pinpoint your message.)

Dr. John R. Brinkley was able to accomplish all of the above. Certainly, being a "doctor" gave him the credibility he needed (to propose the preposterous and be taken seriously), yet no matter the era, there were and are still physicians today whose patient list is meager. Brinkley added as the great motivational guru of his time Napoleon Hill labeled it, *A Little Something More* … himself! As you will read, every facet of his marketing and his business had the Brinkley touch. This leads us to the final piece of the puzzle in helping to generally define his marketing and sales success:

➢ Dr. Brinkley did not hand over the keys to his marketing machine to someone else. If his name was going to be on a marketing brochure or a piece of newspaper or radio advertising, he was going to take a hands-on role. Should any marketer seeking success do less?

With the blueprint now on display, let's take a closer look at John R. Brinkley, the showman, the businessman, and most importantly of all, the master marketer as we reveal *The 21 Principles and Lost Secrets of Dr. J.R. Brinkley-style Marketing!*

*Chip Kessler*

# notes

## *About this book's format*

There are chapters by Chip Kessler, and separate chapters by Dan Kennedy. Each chapter's author is identified.

## *About the Authors*

CHIP KESSLER has lived through many career reincarnations. For over 20 years he was a radio sportscaster covering all major sports. He also did television work, had a book published on college basketball, and has written professionally for sports publications since 1976. At one time he also edited and published a weekly sports newspaper. After leaving the sports life, Chip entered the business world, first in marketing/public relations, and most recently running the day-to-day operations of a healthcare company that develops, produces (and most importantly markets) educational and staff development programs for our nation's assisted living facilities and nursing homes. Two years into this business, he discovered Dan Kennedy and has been a Glazer-Kennedy Insider's Circle™ Member since 2004. Chip credits the teachings of Dan Kennedy and Bill Glazer with dramatically growing his healthcare business activities to the point where he has now also rolled out his first consumer healthcare educational program *"Choices for Care."*

Chip first learned about Dr. John R. Brinkley via Dan Kennedy's recommendation of the book *Charlatan.* He was pleasantly surprised after receiving the book to find out that he was married to a member of John Brinkley's extended family—quickly leading to his wife and other family members' heightened fascination with their rogue relative.

Discover more about Chip at www.ChoicesforCare.com and at www.ChipKessler.com

**DAN S. KENNEDY** is a serial, multi-millionaire entrepreneur, advertising and marketing strategist, and sought after consultant and direct-response copywriter who has brought countless products to market, birthed countless businesses, and made millionaires of many on the strength of his marketing approaches. He is the author of 14 business books, including the popular "No B.S." series published by Entrepreneur Press, the brother of Entrepreneur Magazine, and the *No B.S. Marketing Letter*, which he has written for more than ten years, is the most subscribed to, paid subscription newsletter of its kind. The Glazer-Kennedy Insider's Circle™ membership organization and business empire built on Dan Kennedy's philosophy and ideas encompasses over

25,000 Members, 300,000 online readers, local Chapters meeting regularly in over 100 cities, and international conferences featuring mega-entrepreneur personalities like Gene Simmons (KISS), Joan Rivers and Ivanka Trump. Information about Dan's books can be accessed at www.NoBSBooks.com.

Dan's interest in John Brinkley is particularly piqued by his extensive work in advertising and marketing in the health, alternative health, nutrition and beauty/skin care categories. His significant corporate clients have included Weight Watchers, International, Guthey-Renker and its Pro-Activ® and other skin care brands, and HealthSource, the largest franchise network of chiropractic clinics.

Dan is available for a limited number of speaking engagements and consulting/copywriting assignments. Contact his office via fax: 602-269-3113.

## *Acknowledgements*

The authors wish to express their thanks and gratitude to the Kansas State Historical Society for their assistance in the development of this book, and in particular to Christie Stanley who works in the KSHS Special Collections, Library & Archives Division. Photographs, sample literature and other archive materials presented herein, and in the complete Home Study Course available at ChipKessler.com, are reprinted with permission of the Historical Society. (All rights are reserved and reproduction in any way is prohibited.)

Special thanks as well to Kim Baker for her research into Dr. Brinkley and her many hours of work with the John R. Brinkley archives at The Kansas State Historical Society.

## *Important Resources Note*—**FREE GIFT**

If you're reading this book, you're obviously exceptionally interested in advertising and marketing! We're quite sure you'll love everything that can come your way from Glazer-Kennedy Insider's Circle™ and urge you to explore, beginning with the FREE GIFT available to you, via the offer inside the front and back covers. Why wait until you've finished this book to accept this Gift? Take a minute now to respond at www.Freegiftfrom.com/Kessler.

# an abbreviated background history of Dr. John Brinkley

**D**uring the years of the great Depression, Dr. John Brinkley collected an estimated, astounding $10-million to $20-million from surgeries and patent medicines. He is widely regarded by critics as perpetrator of one of the most outrageous, biggest, and longest running medical frauds in U.S. history. In furthering the promotion of his cure for male sexual dysfunction, Brinkley invented a number of radio broadcasting business breakthroughs. He was much more an advertising, marketing and public relations man than a medical man. His life story is the subject of the New York Times bestselling book *Charlatan* by Pope Brock. This book, *Making Them Believe*, provides in-depth, expert analysis of Brinkley's extraordinarily effective marketing.

## "I HAVE A SCHEME up my sleeve and the whole world will soon hear of it."

*—Dr. John R. Brinkley*

- John Brinkley began has career—can we call it that?—marketing medical cures in 1905.

- In 1918, Brinkley opened his first 16-room clinic in Milford, Kansas.

- By 1920, Dr. Brinkley was attracting national attention, and engaging in nationwide advertising for his goat-glands transplant surgery.

- In 1923, John Brinkley secured one of the first broadcasting licenses in the Midwest, and broke ground on his own radio station.

- In the late 1920's, Dr. Brinkley leveraged his burgeoning fame, and his control of radio programming, to create a network of more than 500 drugstore owners throughout the Midwest, to distribute Brinkley-branded medicines, and service customers driven to them by his radio program, 'The Medical Question Box'.

- In 1930, the trade publication Radio Digest proclaimed Brinkley's KFKB radio station the most popular station in the United States.

- In 1931, he sold KFKB under threat of having its broadcasting license rescinded by the Federal Radio Commission, forerunner to the Federal Communications Corporation, and built his new radio station in Mexico, just beyond the reach of U.S. authorities, but with the wattage to reach listeners throughout the U.S.

- In 1942, in ill health, and in financial difficulty, John Brinkley and his wife Minnie were indicted by federal prosecutors on charges of mail fraud. This, the culmination of decades of pursuit by and combat with the American Medical Association, several federal regulatory and law enforcement agencies, and numerous states' attorney generals.

- John Brinkley died in May 1942.

# the 21 principles of J.R. Brinkley Marketing

# PRINCIPLE #1

PRESENTING YOURSELF WITH

# AUTHORITY

# There's No Substitute for Authority

*By Chip Kessler*

**I**n Dr. Brinkley's time, classic credibility mattered a great deal. Today, new types of credibility, authority and believability apply. People in Brinkley's era, for example, would never have trusted a 'virtual bank' they couldn't walk into, see a huge vault in its corner, and if need be, rush down to, to rescue the money they had on deposit at start of a crisis. But for people who now bank online with an institution that has no physical presence in their community at all, and initially attracts its depositors with television or online advertising, the matter of trust still matters.

**Given a choice, who among us doesn't put our trust and confidence in the man or woman who has relevant, authoritative credentials?** No matter if it is a job around the house that calls for a repairman to visit, or having to place a child into daycare; we want peace of mind that we've made the correct selection from a cluttered field of would-be suitors seeking our business.

In following the examples, which of the choices gives you more confidence that this person can re-wire your downstairs family room?

Mr. Ernie Jones, Electrician

Mr. Ernie Jones, Master Electrician

Who in your mind is more competent to handle the busted pipe that's causing water to cascade onto your bathroom floor?

Mr. Wendell Smith, Plumber

Mr. Wendell Smith, Master Plumber

Finally, you are in need of daycare services for your toddler because both you and your spouse now are working. There are two options to choose from …

The Little Tykes Center

The Red-Robin Pre-School

Which of the above daycares would you call or visit first, based on the name of their respective businesses? Which daycare based upon what you heard and liked would you place your child with and potentially not even visit the competition?

In my little, informal survey, most pick The Red-Robin Pre-*School* - influenced by the word 'school' vs. the word 'center'. Naturally we want the best for our children. We want them to have fun during the day however; we'd also like the idea of them being in an environment that offers structure … and learning. Indeed, both establishments may offer the same exact kind of care, the same activities and structured learning and supervision, but the name "Pre-School" means something to the discerning parent.

As does the title, Doctor. Growing up poor in the hills of North Carolina, John R. Brinkley rapidly came to realize that it was not a lifestyle he wanted to keep. At an early age, and still bound to his home, young Brinkley became captivated by a

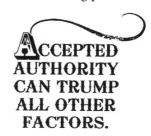

**ACCEPTED AUTHORITY CAN TRUMP ALL OTHER FACTORS.**

traveling medicine show and the "Doctor" Burke that dispensed his brand of "cure-all in a bottle". The cash that flowed to Burke from excited customers that were enamored of the Doctor's message was a message young Brinkley had clearly received. John Brinkley recognized something very important while observing the Doctor peddling patent medicines from the back of a wagon: accepted authority could trump incongruous elements and gain acceptance for just about any promise, however outrageous. Even though people generally associated doctors and medical care with small, professional offices and clinics, if a man were accepted as "Doctor", he could stand on a wood box at the back of a wagon and persuade people to buy the cure for what ailed them. John also saw that 'sales' was path to prosperity, thus, as soon as he was able to go out on his own, John Brinkley would take to the road to perform in such surroundings himself.

## *Creative, Construction Dissatisfaction, Acted Upon*

Not only was Brinkley a quick and eager student of this craft –a very early form of what my co-author, Dan Kennedy, has plied so profitably:

platform selling, John was willing to invest the time and energy to learn more than the basics, and ultimately to elevate his game to a whole new level. He wasn't just satisfied in being a mere medicine show "Doctor" peddling a "one bottle for whatever ails you cure." Rather, his mind-set was to expand his product line, and with it his base of customers. His strategy was brilliant: not only niche out your target market, but within your target market, sub-niche, and build out your line of products to match each sub-niche. In other words why sell everyone attending a medicine show the same one-size-fits-all-cure, when you can identify problems A, B, C and D separately, and then offer a cure specific to each individual ailment. Undoubtedly, only the color of the liquid in bottles A, B, C and D changed; the potion itself was the same. But the price at which it was sold could be higher because it was specialized, the desire for something precisely formulated to cure A by a sufferer of A was greater, many people suffered from more than one malady and would therefore buy two medicines rather than one, and—here's the cleverest part—the very fact of having precisely formulated medicines for different maladies graced Dr. Brinkley with more authority.

I have just named four different, important advantages in the radical change John Brinkley made to the traveling medicine show business and the doctor's pitch. It's worth taking a minute to go back and identify each of the four, and then stop and think of ways you might apply them to your business, profession or industry.

**Even though he literally re-invented the medicine show and made it a much better business, John Brinkley wasn't satisfied with simply being a medicine show doctor.** He yearned for the prestige and credibility of being the "real thing." He foresaw untold advantage of being able to present himself as a real doctor, with credentials from a recognized medical school. However, becoming a doctor through the usual channels wasn't of interest to him. In Brinkley's money making focused mind, this path was too long and tedious. After all, he wasn't actually after the expertise—just the credentials... an early nod to the idea later enunciated and accepted as fundamental premise of advertising: perception *is* reality.

He ventured to Chicago and selected as his school of choice the *Bennett Electric Medical College.* Its so-called physicians preached herbal remedies as the best means to treat a medical problem. Needless to say, the AMA (American Medical Association) thumbed its nose at such practices. For Brinkley, however, both in the price and the less intensive course load, this type of medical degree was exactly what he was after. The school's entry fee was $25, which he plunked down in 1908 to become the college's newest enrollee. And yet John Brinkley was not to earn a degree. With a year to go, he quit school. Even this school's study requirements proved too great for a man in such hurry. Perhaps it was the strain of working a full-time job and also taking class that decided this matter. Another theory offered by author Pope Brook in *Charlatan:* "To a certain kind of mind, graduation is cheating."

In any case, although he dropped out of the *Bennett Electric Medical College,* Brinkley did not abandon what he had learned there, nor his plan to take his place among the nation's most influential names in the field of medical healers. In fact, he sought a fast track. He headed from Chicago to Knoxville, Tennessee and a reunion with his original mentor, Dr. Burke of medicine show fame. Here, John obtained a crash course on the finer points of attracting willing and paying customers, more practical knowledge than his time spent in the legitimate school for would be Electro Medical Physicians.

Ultimately, John Brinkley concluded that formally issued and obtained credentials could be replaced with self-granted credentials and self-promotion. He had come full circle, to perception-is-reality, realizing that most people accept you as you present yourself. From that point forward, whether his name was John R. Brinkley or not (along there way there was the use of an alias or two) the man hailing from Beta, North Carolina always introduced himself as Doctor.

In time incidentally, John Brinkley did get his "medical degree." For one so shrewd and cunning, it wasn't too hard to figure out how to add the one final piece in his search for credibility. He simply bought his degree in 1915 courtesy of the Eclectic Medical University of Kansas City, Missouri. The price: $100 and with it, he was instantly "licensed" to practice in eight states.

What might we conclude from his on-again, off-again desire for actual degree and license to practice medicine? Credentials without aggressive, effective promotion languish in frames on the walls of many a starving professional's office. Aggressive, effective promotion absent legitimate credentials is always a bit fragile and vulnerable to attack. All things considered, possessing both is best.

# 2

# In Search of Maximum Authority

*By Dan S. Kennedy*

**C**hip has identified three chief ways by which the amazing Dr. Brinkley sought and created authority for himself. (Did you identify all three for yourself?)

**On entering the business of the traveling medicine show, and the selling of patent medicines from the stage, John Brinkley re-invented both the products and the pitch to provide authority by specialization.** In doing so, he tossed aside the most fundamental, universal norm of that business: the presentation of one magical, powerful, amazing elixir that cured every imaginable ill. Tossing aside this same norm in any number of other businesses over the years has been of comparable breakthrough value. At the time that two guys started their direct-selling company in 1959, the 'rule' of door-to-door cleaning products was also one bottle of glop to clean everything, and they initially followed that approach. Amway began with a bottle of

7

cleaning fluid called L.O.C., for Liquid Organic Concentrate, that cleaned the kitchen, the bathroom, carpet, functioned as laundry soap, as shampoo, even as ingredient for homemade toothpaste. But this was supplemented in short order by a growing array of cleaning products, each for a single purpose. The professions of medicine and law began with practitioners who did everything, but evolved into a specialist for every isolated need—corporate contract law, family law, elder law, and so on, and clever marketers like one of our Glazer-Kennedy Insider's Circle™ Members, Bill Hammond, have invented their own sub-specialties; in his case, Alzheimer's family law. Brinkley set aside the way the business he was in was done, in order to give himself greater authority by (product) specialization. There is definitely a lesson there for everybody.

If I may, I'll tell you a funny story about this specialized product tactic that I'm proud of, but many would think I ought to be ashamed of myself for. Of course, I've been in the advertising business my entire life, so shame is something of a foreign concept. Anyway, I was working with a fledgling, struggling direct sales company in desperate need of any increase in sales to be had, but lacking capital to add new products. One of its slowest sellers was an excellent, aerosol-foam leather cleaner, treatment and polish in one. I created three different labels for the same can. One, for a cleaner, another for a treatment, and a third for the polish to be buffed to gleaming shine, and packaged the three as a "system". Sales leapt up, and distributors and customers alike raved about the unmatched shine and new softness and pliability of their shoes. I imagine the leather was softer and shinier thanks to getting three consecutive applications and rubbings rather than one, but only thanks to that—the goop was the same in all three cans. Based on this discovery, I used the same trick with that company's aerosol weed killer. I made a label for a weed prevention spray, to be applied to the same areas where the weed killing spray was used, immediately afterward, to keep weeds from coming back. Same stuff in both cans. If anybody feels an apology is due, you aren't getting it from me!

This is now a staple strategy in over-the-counter medicines, nutritional products, skin care products, cosmetics, and many others, and I have my suspicions about how small the difference in actual ingredients may be between Tylenol®, Tylenol® for Migraine Headaches, Tylenol® for Back Pain, and Tylenol® Cold and Flu. Today's drug companies and Dr. John Brinkley have more in common than anybody in big pharma's boardrooms would ever admit.

Again, there's a valuable lesson here for any business owner or marketer, should you care to embrace it.

**Another path to authority traveled by Brinkley was placement of self in environments conducive to it.** The very act of standing up on a stage in front of an audience and confidently and persuasively delivering a presentation has always given that person a grant of authority from the assembled audience, and always will. People have been conditioned from childhood to see such persons as authority figures. They've had twelve or more years of school, sitting and listening to their teachers, compelled to learn, memorize and agree with the teachers' presentations—quite often of mere opinions as facts. If they have religious upbringing, they've had similar conditioning through Bible study classes, catechism classes and church services.

To an extent, John Brinkley overcame a disadvantageous place with the authority-giving advantage of public speaking.

Ideally, you want to exercise thoughtful control over your 'place', over your selling environment, so that it strengthens and does not undermine your authority. Most people do not give this enough thought.

Finally, Brinkley gained authority with a credential: Doctor. He first settled for it by self-appointment and proclamation, and later secured it as legitimate title from a recognized institution, albeit one loose in its requirements. Credentials that convey authority come in many shapes, sizes and types. My friend and student, Diana Coutu, has, for her pizza business, numerous 'best pizza' awards and 'chef awards' secured from national and international competition, and features them in her every ad, brochure, menu, web site, even on the lid of the pizza box. Does her having secured these "honors" guarantee the consumer a better-tasting pizza than may be available from a competitor, and at a significantly lower price? Not necessarily. But do these honors persuade some consumers they are getting a better tasting and higher quality pizza? Yes. Do some consumers value the bragging rights of being her customer and serving her award-winning pizza to their friends? Yes. Does having these honors help her sell at premium prices? Yes.

## *Grant Yourself Permission To Create Your Own Credentials*

In my business as a direct-response advertising copywriter, I've long made much of proclaiming that I am the highest fee, most expensive copywriter. It's not a credential bestowed by or secured from any institution or governing body. It's based on my own research, on copywriters' published fees in professional directories and at their web sites, and, as far as I know, it is true. It says much. I have, incidentally, only a high school education—no college, and have no other formally issued credentials related to the practice of advertising. I've very rarely had that questioned. My self-created credential is more powerful.

Similarly, as a professional speaker, I've never bothered to seek or obtain any of the alphabet-soup credentials or awards bestowed by the industry's trade association, the National Speakers Association. My reaction to the process required to be named a Certified Speaking Professional by NSA is pretty much the same as John Brinkley's was, to going through medical school. But one of the reasons I leapt at the opportunity to appear on Peter Lowe's giant traveling seminar, the SUCCESS events, with audiences of 10,000 to 35,000, and former U.S. Presidents and countless celebrities in its cast was its value as a credential. Let's see... 9 years on the #1 seminar tour in America, as featured on 20/20, 60 MINUTES, in TIME and USA TODAY... or Certified Speaking Professional—which credential has more value in the marketplace?

In 1983, I was involved in the launch of a training company for health care practitioners, featuring educational programs sold by a speaker conducting preview seminars city by city throughout the United States and Canada. Beginning with the very first seminar, for the very first 20 doctors in attendance, he was able to reassure them that they were joining "the largest practice-building organization serving chiropractors, dentists, podiatrists and optometrists"—because ours was *the only* company mixing these professionals in the same seminars. Everybody else separated them by profession. We created our own category-of-one credential.

I think the most important point of all this is that you can—and should—create your own authority, and create and bestow your own credentials for yourself. If you have or acquire any from others, by all means, make the most use of them that you can. But never hesitate to create your own, and never feel handicapped by the lack of credentials granted by others.

# PRINCIPLE #2

## CONVERTING IDEAS TO
# ACTION

# ③

# Turning Ideas into Action

## By Chip Kessler

**T**he great chronicler of 20<sup>th</sup> century business and motivational success Napoleon Hill said it best, *"Thoughts are Things."*

The human mind is an amazing tool. Not a day goes by that our minds aren't filled with thoughts and ideas. For our purposes, let us center on the business and moneymaking "ideas" that come floating from our brain. Sadly, the overwhelming majority of people doesn't recognize a sound idea when it enters their thoughts, let alone have the courage of their convictions to act on what has occurred to them. It's as if the idea has no more importance to them than yawning or scratching an itch.

Certainly some moneymaking ideas were initially thought-up, devised and acted on by the man or woman who was able to conceive the concept in the first place. However, can we honestly say that every successful moneymaking endeavor was initially put in place by the person that was fortunate enough to dream it up? Alas, it isn't so. Almost everybody has had the experience of seeing a product appear on a shelf or in a TV commercial, or a new business open, and then say to themselves: *well, I thought of that years ago.* In truth, there are likely thousands who've thought of every product, service, business or moneymaking opportunity before the first person both thought of it and acted on it.

You might consider how quick you are to dismiss an idea. How slow you are to act on an idea. How creative you are to apply an idea to your business.

Dr. John R. Brinkley was indeed an idea man. However most importantly he was a man of action. An idea without the necessary thrust behind it becomes stillborn in the brain and then leaves our skull. Oh it may linger in our mind for a day. Maybe a week or even a month but soon enough it drifts away.

## *Focused Action Can Be More Powerful*

Armed with his experience as a medical pitchman and his newly purchased license to "practice medicine" John R. Brinkley was ready to create his fortune. He would proceed **based on a single key idea: narrowing his focus to a very particular type of customer/patient, and presenting a very specific solution to a very specific problem.** This flew in the face of just about everything occurring in the legitimate medical community and in the fringe, patent medicines and traveling-doctor/pitchman businesses. All others followed the broad approach, presenting themselves as having every answer to everyone's every need.

From the earliest documentation of John R. Brinkley's business activities, the good doctor concentrated his efforts on one common theme: male function and vitality.

He had other options. Take a few seconds to dwell on all of the medical mysteries he could have concentrated on. Here are a few that even in the first quarter of the 20th century would have been worth his consideration:

Baldness (Even back then as today, men going bald were already receptive to any number of cures on the market).

Weight loss

Lack of Sleep

Poor Circulation

Headache

Backache

Stomach Ache

Tooth Ache

Feeling Run Down

**RESOURCES**

*For information about The Brinkley Secrets Home Study Course, visit ChipKessler.com*

**John Brinkley ignored all of these common, commonly understood, and commonly talked about maladies in favor of one far removed from polite conversation, capable of evoking a much stronger emotional response**. And yet, Brinkley's decision to focus on male function and vitality could also be tied-in to the list presented as a related matter. In other words, implicit in Dr. Brinkley's idea, conquer the big problem and all the smaller ones will topple as well because to the male mind a healthy sex life made up for a lot of ills.

Because of this, Brinkley's marketing efforts (examples to follow) were able tap into one or a few of these by-products of a man's less than stellar vigor. He did not, in fact, sacrifice outreach to people with these common complaints at all. He just got to them through a different path, initially all his own.

Dwell on the words "male function and vitality", as Brinkley did. Even in the 20th century's first quarter almost a hundred years ago, just as it is during this century's first decade with the modern day pitches for the likes of Viagra® and Cialis®, what Dr. Brinkley was selling had to do with a man's performance in bed. Some products (and their messages) truly stand the test of time, because the emotions related to them are evergreen and universal.

Thus his marketing concentrated on the following emotions (and the normal mental thought process of those in need of the Brinkley cure) found in just about every man walking the face of the earth no matter the day, the time or the year:

Ego - Pride

Shame - Embarrassment

Confidence—Worry over Inadequacy and Inferiority

Fear of Failure

Frustration

Anger

Desire to Attract Women

Desire to Satisfy Women

Need to be Loved

Quite a list to work with for any marketer with "the answer" to these human needs and feelings! But that is the point—giving yourself such a good list to work with, and enabling yourself to tap into the strongest possible emotions.

**With his idea clear in his own mind:** who he would target as his market… what emotions of theirs he would appeal to… what problem of theirs he would address and what anxiety he would magnify and exploit… John Brinkley launched massive, aggressive action on many fronts, to quickly become the most famous, and controversial, medical man of his time. We'll start looking at all these actions, as we progress through this book. But don't lose sight of the importance of the core ideas as foundation of and focus for the action, nor the importance of the action in successfully converting the ideas to money. One side of the equation without the other is almost value-less.

# ④

# Fire.
# Aim.

*By Dan S. Kennedy*

**T**here is that joke about the entrepreneur's approach: *Ready.*
*Fire. Aim.* Its humor is in its accurate depiction of far too
many entrepreneurs. In my consulting work, I encounter
this sin of 'blind archery' all too often, acted out in more ways than
could be catalogued in an entire book. In different ways, the majority of
entrepreneurs and marketers are engaged in too much unfocused action.

As example, it's very common to find an entrepreneur or company
spending sizeable sums, exerting enormous effort, utilizing an ever
expanding array of media in pursuit of new customers, with little or no
regard for who, specifically, is or should be the *specific* customer sought—
based on relative and comparative value. This is unfocused investment
and unfocused action.

One of the things I was most impressed with, when I discovered
and began learning about John Brinkley, was his focus. At a time when

the entire business landscape was made up of general practitioners—the family doctor, the general store, etc.—and specialization virtually unheard of, Brinkley developed a very clearly defined idea of his target and his message, built around a single specialty, and stayed with it rigidly and doggedly. His laser focus was remarkable.

**This, I think, is an unsung cause of failure in many, many businesses**. They either begin and grow without focus, or lose focus and drift away from what brung them to the dance over time. Starbucks is a contemporary example of the drift, and the penalty the marketplace can exact for it. Over a few years, breakfast food items were added that were akin to those found all sorts of other, lesser places—from Dunkin Doughnuts to McDonalds, and that stunk up the joint when cooked, over-powering the aroma of the coffee. Stores were opened willy-nilly, in locations that did not fit the original, brilliantly conceived, triangulated, 3rd place between work and home philosophy. Other deviant drift occurred. Gradually, Starbucks ceased to have clear, profound meaning for its core customers. Its founder, Howard Schultz, rushed back in, to try to stop the company from drifting, and restore its focus.

As you get to know Dr. John Brinkley and examine not only his marketing strategies but the examples of his advertising included in this book, and the many more included in The Brinkley Secrets home study course, you will see very little drift, and very clear focus maintained from start to finish, over a long term. His success, ultimately torpedoed only by his growing criminality and a rising regulatory system, stands as testament to this focus—specifically to…

## *Clarity about the target.*

Brinkley was very clear about who he was targeting (and who he was not), and about why he was targeting them, and why they were his ideal customers. Significantly, he was willing to toss aside huge segments of the population in favor of focus. He obviously discarded the entire female gender, except as conduit to their husbands—despite the fact that, at the time, over 80% of all patent medicines, cures, and medical treatments were purchased by women for their personal use. He believed he had good reason to defy these odds, and he was right. He also set aside the population of young, virile men. His target was gender and age specific, and within that, ailment/condition specific, and within that mind-set specific.

Frankly, few business owners are as clear about their target as Brinkley was, and even fewer are willing to stick to that target. Most are easily led astray, led wherever media takes them, led by short-term economics, led by laziness.

## *Clarity about the proposition.*

Brinkley crafted, advanced, and stuck with a single, very focused proposition—in his case, that he could restore youthful, sexual vitality and stamina to any man of any age via one method; the only method that actually worked; which he had perfected. Again, few business owners are as clear about their proposition as Brinkley was, and even fewer are willing to stick to that clear, focused proposition.

**Despite its on-the-surface outrageousness, its controversy, its criticism from peers, professional societies and media, despite all**

**opposition from non-customers, Brinkley stuck to his goat gland
cure for impotence and diminished desire, through thick and thin,
taking measure of its worth only from his target market.** This, too,
is something most businesspeople cannot seem to do. Most are buffeted
about by winds of opinion and criticism from all sides and all sources,
and react to it democratically. I have, for example, never once gone
and read any of the criticism and gossip about me that I know to be
proliferate all over the Internet's chat rooms, web sites, and social media.
I couldn't be less interested in it; because I am convinced the sources of
it are not my good customers or candidates to be good customers. Few
people actually building businesses and reading Investor's Business Daily
and taking care to associate with productive people and profitable ideas
have time to read gossip at Twitter. Yet I know quite a few entrepreneurs,
marketers, authors and consultants who obsess over and are affected by
this kind of gossip about them. The man who holds the record for the
longest run in the same play on Broadway, Yul Brenner, said that he
never read the critics' reviews during his career, because "critics don't buy
tickets." This is how I've always felt, and it is clearly how John Brinkley
operated. Pardon the pun.

# PRINCIPLE #3

## COURAGEOUS PERSONAL
# PROMOTION

# 5

# The Whole of the Sum

*By Chip Kessler*

**A**great marketer avoids the trap of utilizing just one or two methods to get his or her message out to people. It was true before Dr. John R. Brinkley burst onto the scene and it is true today. The only thing that has changed since Brinkley's time is the tools we use in this day and age, and the fact that there are more media resources available to us as marketers than ever before.

Rather than begin by telling you what Brinkley did utilize in order to spread the gospel about himself and his cure, let us first list everything that he didn't have in his marketing tool box: television, the internet, e-mail, Facebook, Twitter, other social media, Amazon, e-books, YouTube, viral video, fax, broadcast fax, the vast commercially available databases and mailing lists, and, well, the list is long, and longer by the day. But what John Brinkley did was utilize every significant media resource available at the time, and pioneer new ways of using them. To use a cliché, he left no stone unturned. As you'll see, he made extensive use of:

Direct Mail

Newspaper advertising

Radio advertising—including his own 'programs'

Film

Books

Speaking before interested audiences

Publicity

Later within these pages, we will delve deeper into the specific methods employed, but suffice to say for our purposes here that John R. Brinkley was not content with merely placing an advertisement in a local newspaper, or running a commercial on a local radio station. Instead, Brinkley's marketing breakthrough was to control both the message itself and the means of how it was delivered. To not only use media, but to own it.

We see this concept practiced today, though perhaps in a more polished fashion. Take for example, Donald Trump's very successful television show, *The Apprentice*, followed by *The Celebrity Apprentice*. While no one can argue the program's entertainment value and that there can be some valuable marketing lessons learned from each episode, the show also serves as a strategic means for "The Donald" to further his own brand, whether it is in his business dealings and/or to add to his status and recognition as an authority figure. Can there be any doubt that the savvy Mr. Trump has benefited business-wise from such national television exposure? Likewise, his number of best-selling books and occasional appearances on the lecture circuit only add to his status as one of the reigning experts in his fields of business and finance. If Donald

Trump's core business is real estate, his second business brand licensing, it shouldn't go unnoticed that his third business is the media business, and his over-arching business is being Donald Trump.

The same can also be said (for its own specific intended consequences) for former Arkansas Governor and 2008 Republican Presidential candidate Mike Huckabee. These days, Mr. Huckabee spends his time as a television personality on the *Fox News Cable Channel.* In addition his *Huckabee Report* is broadcast daily on radio stations across the United States. As well, Governor Huckabee keeps a busy schedule of personal speaking engagements all over the nation, with additional personal appearances promoting the books he has authored. What is the purpose for his extremely busy and challenging calendar of events and activities? It isn't hard to figure out for the expert marketer. He ranks high on the list of preferred GOP Presidential candidates among likely Republican voters for the 2012 election, and he hasn't given up on his ambition. Mike Huckabee certainly knows that in politics, keeping one's name before the public has become a full-time job. No place is this more evident than in the Presidential sweepstakes. The prospective Presidential candidate can no longer wait until a few months before his or her party's Presidential state primaries or caucuses to throw their name out there for consideration. A good example of this was the case of former U.S. Senator Fred Thompson from Tennessee. The lawyer turned actor turned politician turned actor turned politician entered the GOP field rather late in the game with hopes of garnering his party's nomination in 2008. His late entrance soon turned into an early exit. One of the key factors here was the fact that despite Thompson having decent name recognition it wasn't strong enough when compared to the likes of the eventual Republican nominee Senator John McCain or several others in the field of candidates, including Mike Huckabee. The marketing lesson here: timing still matters, but what Dan Kennedy calls 'omnipresence' is far more reliable and powerful. It's best to be visible to your target audience as much as possible, as often as possible, in as many places (media) as possible.

Whether Governor Huckabee again runs for President and if he does, then goes on to gain his party's nomination or not, will play itself out down the road. However for marketing purposes, his active participation media-wise is already paying dividends towards his potential future goal of White House aspirations. He's in the game by virtue of media exposure. As is former Alaska Governor Sarah Palin, via bestselling book, appearances everywhere—even in 'enemy territory' like *Oprah,* on FOX, etc. It probably even helps more than hurts for her to be the brunt of jokes on Leno, Letterman and SNL, and subject of criticism and derision on MSNBC.

Dr. John R. Brinkley had aspirations too. And some 80 years before a Mike Huckabee, Sarah Palin, Donald Trump or any number of the media and marketing savvy personalities we see parading in front of our eyes and ears, there was John R. Brinkley doing whatever it took to sell himself and his cure. He stayed more targeted in his outreach, but still used every media, and fought for constant exposure to the public eye.

# In The Business of Being Dr. John R. Brinkley

*By Dan S. Kennedy*

**W**hat business is **Martha Stewart** *really* in? She receives money from many products, services and businesses, a few directly, many via licensing. Money flows to her from dishes, pillowcases and blankets, furniture, apparel, gardening tools, books, DVD's, magazines, and TV programs. Money comes to Martha from Macy's Department Stores, from Home Depot, from Barnes & Noble, from the Hallmark cable TV channel, as well as from speaking and personal appearance fees. But what business is she really in? The Martha Stewart business.

This is something John Brinkley understood, and was quite willing to do; he was in the Dr. John Brinkley business.

Of course, there are plenty of successful corporations, enterprises and products that do not have a human face and are not attached to a human personality. Conversely, though, many huge corporations and magnificently successful businesses are. Or at certain key times are. Walt

Disney personally made Disney popular with America, and Walt is still an ever-present part of Disney marketing all these years after his death. The first time Chrysler was brought back from bankruptcy's brink, it was its Chairman, Lee Iacocca who personally sold the company to America, and interestingly, as a by-product, made himself an immensely popular celebrity-CEO, leading to two bestselling books, audio and video products, and speaking engagements after his Chrysler years. Dave Thomas built Wendy's on a character based on his daughter, and later spurred its greatest growth by becoming its face, and starring in its TV commercials, somewhat reluctantly. It's worth noting that Dave was mentored in the restaurant business by Colonel Sanders.

At the small business level, it is my contention that human personality is much more critical, and an even greater percentage of stellar successes feature a promotable and heavily promoted person, not a nameless, faceless, inhuman institution. Admittedly, there is more than one way to approach this and be successful, but I steer most of my clients into putting a person in the spotlight, not a company.

**FROM THE BRINKLEY BLUEPRINT:** *Being in the business of You*

The John Brinkley blueprint has certainly been used, nearly in its entirety, by other, more contemporary individuals around whom large companies and enduring brand names have been built. If you'll take time to research Dr. Atkins, you'll find that, at his peak, he was very much a modern day John Brinkley. He was focused, promoting a single, simple, radical proposition: that everything about diet including the time-honored food pyramid and balanced approach was wrong; that simply slashing carbs would provide quick and sustained weight loss and better overall health. He was a controversial personality, criticized and attacked by the medical establishment, regulatory bodies and the media, but never wavered. He was a lightning rod, so he got tons of media exposure. He promoted himself relentlessly. And the Atkins brand lives on and thrives long after his death. To some extent, his positions on weight loss and diet, and carbs not calories or fat as enemy, have gained broader if grudging acceptance in recent years, particularly with regard to prevention or treatment of diabetes, in part a disease of obesity. I have no idea whether or not Atkins studied Brinkley, but if you Google®, Wikipedia® and gather information about Atkins and samples of early Atkins advertising, articles, interviews and books and compare them to Brinkley's, the parallels are obvious and comprehensive.

In the arena of personal finance, a study of Dave Ramsey's marketing of himself and development of his media, businesses and income streams will reveal the Brinkley blueprint.

In religion, Rev. Ceffalo Dollar. And, with more moderate tonality, Rev. Rick Warren.

This 'Brinkley blueprint' for personal promotion that I'm referring to has three key elements I should call your attention to. One is the advancement of a clear, focused and usually a shocking or radical or contrarian proposition. A linked second is deliberate controversy. Third, being about something and known for that thing. Fourth is the exploitation of that created personality through every possible media that can get one in front of his target audience. Fifth, not just using media, but when possible, owning it.

Personally, I've long been in *the business of being Dan Kennedy*, and I think of myself as comparable to Martha Stewart as well as John Brinkley. I get money from many products, services and sources, some directly, most indirectly. I get money from books, info-products, newsletters, memberships, events, and from relationships with five different publishers. I also get money from speaking fees, appearance fees, consulting fees, and copywriting fees. But I am in the business of being me and promoting me. I suppose it's a "thin" business, but I have twice created saleable equity and sold entities based on it. I promote myself personally or have myself promoted by partners utilizing a wide variety of media, including books, newsletters, web sites, e-mail, social media, print media advertising, direct-mail, radio interviews, columns and articles,

**FROM THE BRINKLEY BLUEPRINT:**
*Clear, focused, often shocking proposition*
*Deliberate controversy*
*Purpose or mission: being* ABOUT *something*

syndicating content to hundreds of newsletter publishers. Not using radio or TV is result of failed attempts, not lack of trying. And I developed owned media; first my own, now in the hands of Glazer-Kennedy Insider's Circle™; our media platform includes three main newsletters, e-mail publications (reaching, at last count, over 300,000), audio programs, and much more.

Of course, the local shop owner can be quick to decry all of this. *I own a local cupcake store and none of this applies to me.* Brinkley could have had a small, local practice with all his patients in a 20-mile radius, and lived an invisible life too. He just chose not to. And had patients travel from all over the continent to come to him. These days, boundaries have been erased for all kinds of businesses—even cupcake stores—so I'd urge thinking bigger. Global, not local. But even if you resist that, you ought to realize that any business can be boosted by its owner being famous and endlessly fascinating at least to its target market, if not to the entire community.

# PRINCIPLE #4

## UNABASHED PROMISE OF A
# CURE

# 7

# Offering a Cure

*By Chip Kessler*

I**t's a formula that has paid dividends time after time *as just the word alone* will often make a somewhat disinterested party sit up and take notice: *cure!*** Think of the word cure as in "curious". The idea of a cure—especially a simple, easy, quick, permanent cure—arouses great curiosity, because it so concisely summarizes what everybody wants, finds elusive, yet buys hopefully again and again. Unhappy people want *to be made* happy. Overweight people want to be made thin. Poor people want to be made rich. For whatever ails, frustrates, torments, troubles, mystifies or plagues, there is the hope that there is *a* cure.

As has often been stated by my co-author, Dan Kennedy, people are *not* looking for prevention; they are looking for the cure! They are *not* eager to look to themselves and their own thoughts, attitudes, skills, behavior, or initiative, effort, discipline, diligence and persistence for that cure either. They are looking in their medicine cabinet or pharmacy, to some wizard, for a magic pill or phrase or gadget. They are not likely to be patient, either. They want whatever ails them, their family, home or business cured for them, and cured fast.

John Brinkley understood all this, innately, and from his observation of the patent medicine pitchman's pitch, and from his earliest experiences. When he developed his core ideas about what business to be in and what proposition to advance, he did not choose the treatment business, the behavior modification business or the education business. He chose the cure business. He let his audience know that he had the cure for the problem(s) that ailed them. His success in persuading people of the fact of his instant and permanent cure was such that the doctor could name his own price and get it. Could draw patients from far and wide, and have them travel great distances. For all of the first three decades of the 1900's, John Brinkley sold The Cure.

In the beginning, John Brinkley merely made incremental improvements to commonly sold herbal remedies and patent medicines, and pitched them in a more persuasive manner. But he was on the hunt for something that could transcend all such products and be presented as a revolutionary, transformative cure. This occurred to him early, but it took a bit of time to settle on it. **The salient question for every business owner to contemplate is: what can I find, create, re-position and present as The Cure for what ails my customer?**

**HIGH VALUE QUESTION:** *how can YOU present THE Cure for what ails your customer?*

At the moment, there is a pretty effective advertising campaign for a travel destination, presenting it as The Cure for a dull, boring, and apparently sexless marriage. It's not carried out as dramatically as I'd imagine John Brinkley doing it, but it's there. There is a very successful direct-response print and radio advertising campaign running as of this writing, promising parents an easy, instant cure for disrespectful, ill-behaved, impossible to control children. It's a campaign John Brinkley would love. In every business, there is the potential to convert to selling 'The Cure'.

Dr. Brinkley's paramount breakthrough, product-wise, came shortly after he moved to the town of Milford, Kansas in 1917. Brinkley, practicing his personal brand of herbal remedies, had hung out his shingle and patients began trickling in. One in particular, a local farmer, complained of a lack of pep in general and a loss of sexual vitality; both conditions were old Brinkley mainstays. One thing led to another and the idea was offered between physician and farmer of an instant and permanent cure by transplantation of a goat's testicles into the man's scrotum. The surgery was soon performed. A couple of weeks later, the farmer returned with the good news. Perhaps the only resident of Milford more pleased that the farmer—and maybe the farmer's wife*—was Dr. John R. Brinkley. The farmer was more than happy to spread the word and other locals soon followed onto Brinkley's operating table. A testament to the power and persuasion of a personal testimonial from the heart, and how it instantly gave Dr. Brinkley a niche that would carry him and his reputation to fame, or as others would label it, infamy.

(*The farmer's wife was so pleased with her husband's newly found sexual prowess that she asked Dr. Brinkley to outfit her with a matching set of goat ovaries.)

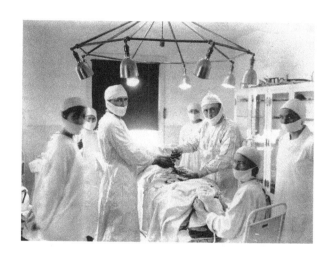

HERE THEY ARE: *Dr. John Brinkley and his surgical team, presumably in the midst of goat glands transplant surgery.*

# 8

# Choose To Sell What People Want

*By Dan S. Kennedy*

**T**he advice in this Chapter's title sounds ridiculously simple, doesn't it? And it is. But still, it is rarely adhered to!

Coca-Cola® was once sold as a cure for low energy, fatigue and listlessness. Its original formula contained a bit of cocaine, so it probably fulfilled the advertised promise. Vibrators were originally administered to women by physicians in their offices, as a cure for female moodiness and depression. Marketers in the health, alternative health, diet fields somewhat naturally understand the power of promising cures, although evermore restrained in straightforwardly doing so by laws and regulations. People in most other fields don't usually think of themselves as being in the business of selling a cure—but they should.

I've embraced this idea just about my entire business life. On my own behalf or for clients, I've advertised and sold the cure for uncertain, roller-coaster income; the cure for sales slumps; the cure for below-par farm harvests; the cure for golfers' yips and slices; the cure for humiliating acne break-outs; the cure for Weight Loss Resistance Syndrome®; the cure for entrepreneurial loneliness. And on and on. If you'll take a fresh look at my famous Giorgio letters for an Italian restaurant (in the *Ultimate Sales Letter* book, or in *The Magnetic Marketing System*), you'll see that not only aren't they about dining out in a restaurant, they are actually about a cure for a marital problem. If you listen to my 'million dollar speech' that sold Magnetic Marketing, you'll find it opens by promising cures for very frustrating ailments, one for sales professionals, a different one for business owners. Actually, you'll be hard-pressed to examine any of the advertising or marketing I've created for myself or for clients that doesn't promise a cure, or at least allude to one.

**FROM THE BRINKLEY BLUEPRINT:** *Certainty.*

John Brinkley was obviously utterly unrestrained and unabashed in promising The Cure, in no uncertain terms. It is, as I often point out, easier to be that strong and straightforward and grandiose if you suspend any requirement to tell the truth and I do not advocate outright fraud. There's almost no sum of money sufficient to pay for many nights sharing bunk beds in a concrete block cell, with a serial killer named Bruce. However, Brinkley had it right, conceptually. By that I mean, it's up to you to find a way to be as forceful, bold, dramatic and clear as you possibly, legally can be, in holding out promise of The Cure to what ails your target customers. Subtlety or even reasonableness is not rewarded.

There is something even more important than his cure that John Brinkley sold. It, more than the goat testicles nonsense, made him rich and famous. By whatever process of observation, intuition, experimentation and experience that led him to it, Brinkley hit upon and very successfully promoted the thing people want above all else. *Certainty.*

He was entirely unambiguous. He promised, actually guaranteed certain results. The *certain* cure.

This does not just apply narrowly to the clarity and strength of whatever guarantee you attach to your products or services, although it certainly does apply to that. In a bigger, broader sense, it applies to who you present and promote yourself as, and how you position and present your products and services. Just as nobody lines up to see the wise man *at the bottom of* the mountain, no one lines up to consult the uncertain, ambiguous psychic either. We don't want to hear the word "maybe" when buying psychic predictions. Or medical diagnosis. Or expert advice. We just don't.

As you study the actual copy in John Brinkley's literature, listen to or read transcripts of his radio broadcasts, and otherwise delve into his presentation of self and cure, you'll find the golden thread of *absolute certainty.*

# PRINCIPLE #5

## SELL DEEPER

# MEANINGS

# 9

# There's Nothing You Can't Get If You Help Others Get What They Want

*By Chip Kessler*

**I**t's as simple a success principle as there is. The legendary Zig Ziglar has had a long and successful career and in no small part has attributed his accomplishments to the phrase: "You can get everything in life you want if you help enough people get what they want."

This thought didn't begin and end with Zig Ziglar. He took it from the Bible, and gave it only a slight re-write. It didn't first appear in the thought process of Dr. John Brinkley either but he was one of the leading champions of this philosophy in his day, writing and lecturing about it publicly, and, privately, telling close confidantes that he was selling and giving people what they really wanted—confidence, so he deserved all the acclaim and wealth he created.

Brinkley's product was the transplanting of goat testicles into the male sack and the revolutionary (and documented via testimonials) results that had occurred in his male patients ... due to his surgical techniques and skill. In effect, Brinkley offered the fountain of youth, and was not shy about saying so. The operation may have been bogus, despite the copious testimonials. But if you deeply analyze what Dr. Brinkley was really selling, it wasn't surgery, and it wasn't even the promised physical effects of the surgery. John Brinkley was giving men self-confidence.

A great many businesses have been built on the same deliverable. The Dale Carnegie empire was built by giving men confidence in business settings, particularly in speaking up and putting across their ideas in meetings. John Brinkley's fortune amassed by giving men confidence in the bedroom.

We have already touched on this subject briefly and now as we begin to really hone in on the marketing strategies and principles that enabled John R. Brinkley to become a magnet for paying customers, it's time to list the core ingredients of the Brinkley marketing message blueprint, as applied to the male population:

*Are you feeling inadequate?*

*Are you insecure?*

*Are you worried about this?*

*Do you feel as if you're now unattractive to your wife?*

*Are you miserable about your inability?*

These are the questions John Brinkley frequently raised in his advertising, radio broadcasts and speeches. By raising such questions, he undermined men's confidence. If it was already lagging, this made it worse. It's the "Agitate" step in Dan Kennedy's Problem+Agitate/Problem+Solution formula. And a good question for you is what questions should you be asking your customers, to agitate their negative emotions and heighten their need or desire for your cure?

Also keep in mind that even though the message was "directed" toward men, what woman out there who was suffering from the end results (or in this case the lack thereof) of her man's sexual inadequacies, wasn't reading and hearing the Brinkley marketing message with a heightened sense of curiosity? In other words, the good doctor was drawing new business from both men that needed what he was offering, and women who needed it for their men.

Brinkley had the best of both marketing worlds. While he was able to niche his marketing message directly to long-suffering males, his communication also hit home with females. Who's to say as well that a man, too embarrassed to step forward and openly profess his need for the "Brinkley cure," wasn't pushed to visit the doctor by his eager, hopeful, sexually frustrated wife?

Amongst the many 'lost secrets' of Brinkley marketing, we can see that the posing of questions that raise and reinforce self-doubt and personal anxiety can be more powerful than the making of assertions and affirmative statements. Some of the greatest classic mail-order/direct-response advertisements of all time-share this approach. Worthy of your research*, for example, are legendary ads and direct-mail campaigns bearing these headlines:

- Do You Make These Mistakes In English?

- Does Your Child Ever Embarrass You?

- Are You Just A Hair Shade Away From Looking Younger And Prettier?

- How Many Of These Common Gardening Mistakes Are Causing You To Work Harder Than You Really Have To?

- Have You Ever Felt Lonely—Even With Other People Around?
  ... Or asked yourself: "Is this all there is for me?"

- Are You Ashamed Of The Smells In Your House?

The arousal and agitation of feelings of inadequacy, being looked down by others, failing to measure up—whether in the bedroom, bank account or backyard gardening—is a very reliable strategy from which John Brinkley extracted a fortune. You can too.

*Relevant reference books: *How To Write A Good Advertisement* by Schwab; *Twenty Ads That Shook The World*/Twitchell; *The Greatest Direct-Mail Sales Letters Of All Time*/Hodgson

# 10

# An End
# To Selling 'Stuff'

*By Dan S. Kennedy*

**P**eople think about their businesses in ways that sabotage rather than elevate. How you think about yourself and your business can be imprisoning or liberating, small or big, trivial or important or *profoundly* important, ordinary or exceptional, competitive or unique, innovative or repetitive, focused on your deliverables or focused on their meaning, you choose how you think. Those choices ultimately control how others think about you. This is no small thing!

If John Brinkley had thought of himself as a doctor—really, or as a surgeon, or as having a medical practice, or in any, way, shape or form, in terms of the core product or service he provided, it's extremely unlikely we'd be writing this book about him. Brinkley certainly thought bigger than most, bolder than most, on a more epic scale than most. But most importantly, he thought in terms of customer wants, not in terms of goods or services.

This sounds quite simple. As I re-read the last sentence of that paragraph, I thought to myself: heck, everybody'll instantly react: *well, that's nothing new. I already know that.*

Admittedly, it's nothing new, although it was pretty darned revolutionary in John Brinkley's days of ascendancy. I write about it constantly, there's some mention of it in virtually every book I've ever written. Much of the *Uncensored Sales Strategies* book I contributed to, chiefly written by former, infamous Mayflower Madam, Sydney Barrows is about this idea. The latest way I've been talking about it is in terms of being product-centric vs. customer-centric. My consulting work with private clients has featured this for over 25 years. No, it's nothing new.

And maybe you do know it. But I often point out, the fat doctor who smokes, *knows.* It's not that he was out sick the days they covered obesity, tobacco toxicity and cancer at medical school. It isn't that he didn't get the memo. There's even a warning right on the side of every pack of cigarettes. It's pretty straightforward. It says: these will kill you. He knows about all this. But his knowing hasn't translated into doing. In fact, his behavior is in opposition to his knowledge. That's the way it is with most businesspeople, most advertisers, most marketers. They know what I'm talking about here. But their actions remain in opposition to it.

The thing to be thinking about is: *how can I help my target customers get what they want?* Not: *how the devil can I sell what I've got?* But, most business owners spend most waking moments thinking about selling their stuff, not identifying, understanding and fulfilling wants. Most take a merchandising approach, not a psychological approach.

It's rare to find a marketer as *pure* about this as John Brinkley. It's certainly something to aspire to.

In many venues, for some time, I have been urging people to "stop selling STUFF"—including my books *No B.S. Marketing to the Affluent, No B.S. Sales Success In The New Economy* and *No B.S. Business Success In The*

**HIGH VALUE QUESTION:** *how can you best help your target customers get what they want —and be perceived as doing so?... NOT: how can I sell my stuff?*

*New Economy*, and my newsletters, *No B.S. Marketing Letter* and *No B.S. Marketing to the Affluent.* George Carlin's shtick about this has become reality: everybody simply has way, way, way too much stuff! Their houses are giant storage sheds of stuff, into which they squeeze a bed, toilet and microwave. How much stuff does anybody need? Or even want? We may very well have hit that wall. This was, in my opinion, a contributive factor to the recession that really took hold of America in 2008 and 2009.

We *must* now elevate our game to marketing by values and selling with deeper meanings. Exceptionally successful (as I write this) big companies in touch with this are Disney, Apple, to some extent, Michelin, Subway. Wal-Mart is attempting this transition. Starbucks drifted from it and is trying to return. Every marketer needs to be very aware of this savvy movement away from selling stuff, study it wherever they observe it occurring, and bring it home to their own businesses.

## PRINCIPLE #6

# ELEVATE
### YOURSELF WITH MEDIA

## PRINCIPLE #7

# MULTIPLY
### YOURSELF WITH MEDIA

# 11

# Media,
# Not Manual Labor

*By Chip Kessler*

ohn Brinkley's introduction to the lucrative opportunities in selling patent medicines was observing the traveling medicine shows, with charismatic pitchmen who called themselves doctors but made their money as salesmen. Most real physicians set up shop and built practices, or in some cases, multi-doctor clinics, almost entirely by word of mouth referrals. He followed these models at first, but very quickly gravitated toward means of getting his message out to many more people at a faster pace.

**Dr. John Brinkley also realized that the very nature of his "miracle cure" for male sexual dysfunction would be a subject of intrigue, skepticism and curiosity. He understood that the average person would be curious about it, and most importantly the average person would want to know more about *the man behind* this revolutionary and controversial process.** To use this as leverage, he devised a strategy that has, in contemporary times, been copied by a great many individuals manufacturing fame: not writing a book, but having a book written about him.

There were two of these books:

## *The Life of a Man* by Clement Wood

This was a ghostwritten saga with the Brinkley heavily involved in the development of the manuscript behind the scenes.

## *A Tribute to Dr. John R. Brinkley ... the man without parallel*

The author of the second book was so enamored and reverent towards the good Doctor that he didn't feel worthy enough to give himself a writer's credit. The opening paragraph of the book reads as follows, *"Good evening ladies and gentlemen- boys and girls! I come to you tonight to pay tribute to Dr. John R. Brinkley, a "Man without a Parallel." Of course most of you know of Dr. Brinkley and I am a stranger to you, but I speak not of Dr. Brinkley the great doctor, but of Dr. Brinkley the noble man.*

These books were promoted aggressively, as objective reports on a prominent leader in the field of medicine, and they presented Brinkley as a man on a mission, a daring innovator, and a humanitarian. If you stop to think about it, the very fact that a book has been written about you and published for public consumption means you must be important! Even people who had never before heard of Dr. John Brinkley or his transformative surgical procedures knew instantly that he was an important, interesting person and significant figure they *should* know about, because a book about him had been published.

Use of this unusual strategy did not stop Brinkley from also positioning himself as an author. He self-published *Dr. Brinkley's Doctor Book*, and advertised and sold it for $1.00 a copy—a significant sum in his day.

The books built the credibility and fame of Dr. Brinkley, but, by far, his biggest breakthrough came from the then young medium of radio, beginning with KFKB- *Milford, Kansas, "the Sunshine Station in the Heart of the Nation."*

## Which Media Offers The Best Breakthrough Opportunity FOR YOU?

As the Brinkley name grew, the Brinkley personal magnetism that had worked so well in one-on-one "consultations" with prospective patients would be effective in the most personal of all advertising media, radio. Unlike printed matter, requiring the prospective patient to actively read, thus sacrificing control of tone to the reader, radio enabled Dr. Brinkley to multiply himself, yet still connect one to one, using his trained voice, voice inflections, dramatic pauses and persuasive speaking style just as he had as a medicine show pitchman. Sitting next to his radio, in the comfort of his or her home, a listener could experience the medical wisdom of Dr. John R. Brinkley through his series of medical talks. Of course, just being on the radio gave Brinkley authority, credibility and importance. He was ingenious enough not to run straightforward commercials, but instead to host programs, provide helpful information, and deliver 'fireside chats' about health issues.

The power of radio was immediately evident to John Brinkley, and his ambition naturally escalated. Brinkley didn't just want to be on the radio, he wanted to own a radio station. After all, was there a faster means to add to one's growing authority than to be able to call the shots and be on the air as often as he desired? If he owned his own radio station, he would be able to appear when he pleased to espouse on whatever medical mystery, illness, or disease was out there worthy for his opinion and expertise. Yet even Brinkley, the master marketer of all things realized that wall-to-wall medical discussion, no matter how informative, was not the best means to make his business grow. As mentioned earlier in the book, a Brinkley knows how to "give the people what they want" and in the case of KFKB, this meant first-class musical entertainment. His clever goal was to make his chats stand out amidst a sea of other programming that was attractive to listeners.

As a result, Dr. John R. Brinkley physician and surgeon would also become John R. Brinkley radio program director. He searched the nation far and wide for musical talent, focusing more on the down-home country, folksy style that would be a good match for his personal talent for delivering down-home, folksy, from the heart medical advice. Brinkley acquired a station, created a live music format, and invested mind-boggling sums in bringing entertainers to Milford, Kansas to perform live in his studio. The radio stars that appeared included champion fiddle player Uncle Bob Larkin, Patsy Montana, Red Foley, Gene Autry and Jimmie Rodgers, plus a host of young and upcoming talent that Brinkley was proud to have discovered.

Brinkley would eventually sell KFKB, but not until it had become one of the most popular radio stations in the state of Kansas. At the time of the sale, Brinkley was so popular and what he had to say on the medical subjects of the day so respected that he continued his radio broadcasts under the new ownership, as a legitimized broadcast personality.

A footnote here to Dr. John R. Brinkley's role in radio is that he saw it as such a viable medium for delivering his marketing message that later during his career, when he moved to Del Rio, Texas, and then on to Little Rock, Arkansas, Brinkley made it a point to own radio stations in both locales, the Del Rio operation actually across the boarder in Mexico. One other point of interest: among the acts that Brinkley championed during his radio programmer stints was the "Original Carter Family" a group that would become one of the leading clans in country music. Among the Carter off- spring, a daughter named June who joined the act at a young age and would go on later in life to marry an up and coming country entertainer by the name of Johnny Cash. The "Man in Black" said that he had first heard June sing over the airwaves on a Brinkley radio station.

Not content with the medium of radio, Brinkley also tapped into the film genre producing a short feature film, to be shown in movie theaters: *The Story of Paw and Maw.*

This cautionary story tells the tale of a man named Paw who is suffering from an "ailment." He goes and visits his regular local doctor but the trip doesn't cure him of his problem. Still on the lookout for some relief, Paw next goes to see his local druggist and begins taking a lot of medicine. Sadly the medication doesn't do him any good, so Paw again treks back to his regular physician. The doctor decides that Paw needs an operation. Unfortunately the surgery doesn't cure Paw. In fact the surgery kills him.

As the story unfolds, the viewer sees what Paw should have done:

➤ If only he had been a regular listener of Dr. Brinkley's radio station then Paw would have become familiar with the heralded healer.

➤ If only Paw had also purchased Dr. Brinkley's Doctor Book and followed the sound wisdom and advice between the front and back covers...

➢ If only Paw had boarded a train and gone to see Dr. Brinkley…

➢ If only Paw had heeded the expert counsel Dr. Brinkley would have given him things would've turned out differently.

➢ The final announcement is made in the film under the picture of a hail and hearty Paw standing in front of the Brinkley Hospital, travel bag at his side, coat nattily slung over his right arm and his fashionably styled wide brimmed hat raised in the air triumphantly in his left hand:

> "Paw, like many others would have returned home a healthier and happier man."

In its time, John Brinkley's ambitious media strategy went far beyond what any other promoters of medical care or products—or just about anything else—imagined, but today, we see many entrepreneurs, authors and others using their own radio programs, bought and paid for in many cases; their own books and books they arrange to have written about them; their own magazines and newsletters. There is, of course, a vast array of online media available, so that, in a sense, you can own your own radio station, produce and broadcast your own short films (think: YouTube) as well as full-length webinars, and otherwise produce and deliver programming that demonstrates your expertise and attracts customers.

The Brinkley blueprint for savvy use of media had three parts:

1: Multiplying himself via EVERY available media

2: By doing so, gaining "multi-media reinforcement"

3: Finding and focusing on THE medium best suited to him and his purposes

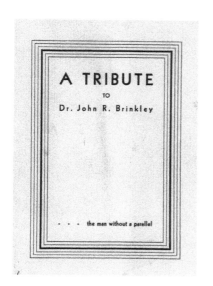

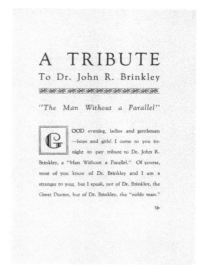

# A TRIBUTE
## To Dr. John R. Brinkley

### "The Man Without a Parallel"

GOOD evening, ladies and gentlemen —boys and girls! I come to you tonight to pay tribute to Dr. John R. Brinkley, a "Man Without a Parallel." Of course, most of you know of Dr. Brinkley and I am a stranger to you; but I speak, not of Dr. Brinkley, the Great Doctor, but of Dr. Brinkley, the "noble man."

*Cover and first page of the "Tribute Book." (The entire book is included along with other samples of Dr. Brinkley literature in the complete Home Study Course available at www.ChipKessler.com)*

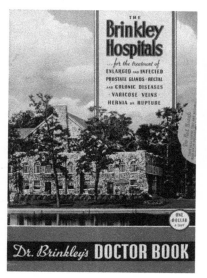

Cover, inside front cover, a text page (page 4) and diagram page (page 5) of "The Dr. Book." (The entire book is included along with other samples of Dr. Brinkley literature in the complete Home Study Course available at www.ChipKessler.com)

# 12

# Why Not You?

*By Dan S. Kennedy*

I admire boldness. And, fortune very often favors the bold.

**Many people use media to limited extent or piece-meal—and too timidly**. The idea of using one's own radio show to dispense information, establish expertise and celebrity, and attract clients or patients pioneered by John Brinkley has become a commonly used, and often, very successful strategy for health practitioners like chiropractors, dentists, even veterinarians, as well as financial planners and investment advisors. In virtually every city, there are at least several of these kinds of 'programs' on local radio stations. Occasionally, you can find someone outside those categories also using this strategy—as example, I know of a martial arts school owner with an hour-long weekly program for parents, about all aspects of raising good kids; a travel agent specializing in luxury tours has a weekly program. An M.D. who I worked with as a private client for several years had a hugely successful, bought and paid for weekly radio program in his local market, and because of it secured a gig as the resident health expert on a network TV station's morning and noon news

**67**

programs, presented twice a day, everyday as the leading authority in his city. Another past client of mine, Dan Frishburg, an investment advisor went from his own bought-and-paid for radio programs to being hired to host a real show on the #1 station in his market, and then, ala Brinkley, bought the station, and organized an entire stable of business, finance and political talkers he owned and controlled, with all on-air promotion supporting his investment practice. The last I visited with him, he was in the process of acquiring a second station in another market. But most entrepreneurs stop far short of a bold, comprehensive, multi-media approach on a scale comparable to John Brinkley's. Most think small and stay small. *Unnecessarily.*

As an aside, let me point out something that John Brinkley did, described in the preceding chapter, but not put under the spotlight. It has been a huge breakthrough for a number of people I've worked with personally, so I have seen its power firsthand. When Brinkley took over his first radio station and recognized he needed other programming to attract and hold listeners, so he could intersperse his programs and have a large audience for them, he invested in bringing popular entertainment celebrities of his time to his radio shows, as well as in turning unknowns into celebrities.

Peter Lowe wiped out dozens of well-established promoters of "success rallies" almost overnight when he invested in top celebrities to star in his events—beginning with former President Ronald Reagan. It was also his purpose to position himself with a star-studded line-up of celebrity speakers to make himself a famous speaker who could command the attention of huge audiences and have his religious message listened to, by people who would otherwise never give him the time of day. I spoke for nine years on his SUCCESS tour, and doing so contributed enormously to my own rise in prominence, reputation and celebrity, so I'm grateful for his boldness and big thinking.

My clients Bill Guthy and Greg Renker forever changed the infomercial business by investing in celebrity hosts. By doing so, they instantly elevated their shows above all others. They made Tony Robbins a major personality by surrounding him with celebrities in infomercials, and they built the #1 brand in acne treatment products with celebrity-driven infomercials and commercials.

Dan Frishberg, who I mentioned above, had the cajones to chase—and get—major celebrities, political and financial world leaders and other experts to be guests, interviewed live, on his original, paid-for ("fake") radio program on a dinky-market station, even including Henry Kissinger and Alan Greenspan, who rarely do radio interviews. Because they were important, he quickly became important, attracting the attention of the real media in his market, as well as the public.

I call this **the strategy of attachment**. What or who you attach yourself to in the public eye is what you are accepted as.

I obviously did not know John Brinkley. I am old, but nowhere near *that* old. But I have gotten to know Glenn W. Turner quite well, and studied him and his business adventures thoroughly—and the parallels between Brinkley and GWT, as he's famously known, are many. In going from zero to attracting over 500,000 followers to his multi-level marketing behemoths, Koscot Kosmetics and Dare to Be Great, in just 3 years, GWT employed just about every media strategy Brinkley pioneered but radio. He hired a retired, Pulitzer Prize winning journalist to write three books about him; he had a feature film made about him and his companies and their epic war with state attorney generals and federal regulators, to be shown in theaters (although it was used most in company events); he surrounded himself with celebrities, including a popular country-western and gospel signing group, The Jordanaires, who wrote and recorded songs about him and about Koscot , released by his own record label, Soundkot. He even recorded one song with them. He also created his own celebrities, including twin midget motivational speakers, John and Greg Rice (who subsequently appeared in the movie *Foul Play* with Chevy Chase and Goldie Hawn). He traversed the country in private jets with his image painted on the tails, and organized giant events resembling rock concerts or political rallies. He cultivated media coverage with controversy, flamboyance, large charitable donations, and, at one point, running for the Florida senate and threatening to run for President (as did Brinkley). He was featured in LIFE MAGAZINE—one of the largest circulation magazines of the time, in hundreds of newspapers, and even in a real book, not subsidized by him, by investigative journalist Rudy Maxa. He vexed his peers in the multi-level marketing industry, enraged government regulators, and ultimately had laws created specifically to put him out of business—a fate also shared by Brinkley. Working on this book has made me wonder why GWT didn't use radio too, and I intend asking him the next time we talk.

Dr. Brinkley and Glenn Turner made themselves *larger than life.*

The list of contemporary business and media personalities who have done the same, and profited enormously, is long, and encompasses just about every category - real estate, finance - Donald Trump; success -Tony Robbins; personal finance—Suze Orman, Dave Ramsey; lifestyle—

Martha Stewart; food—Rachel Ray; conservative politics—Rush Limbaugh, Glenn Beck; relationships and family—Dr. Laura, Dr. Phil. If you will take the time to research the backgrounds of these celebrities, you will find most were once unknown, toiling in oblivion, working in small ponds, and that **they manufactured their own celebrity. So, why not you?**

Brinkley did it at a time of extremely limited media, enormous costs involved in utilizing it, and great logistical difficulties in using it. Glenn Turner, under conditions not as difficult as Brinkley's, but still far more challenging than today's conditions. Brinkley, a man of very limited education, made up credentials, and very questionable propositions. Turner, an 8th grade dropout, handicapped with a speech impediment. If they could, why not you?

To be clear, I am not necessarily suggesting you go as rogue as did Brinkley, or, for that matter, Turner. Certainly not that you commit fraud. However, the qualifications of those on the above list to be leading, celebrated, globally recognized experts in their fields are, to be kind, suspect. Many of them have made up their own credentials, greatly exaggerated them, or simply proceeded without them. Many have skeletons in their closets that contradict their public personas. Puritan Dr. Laura's closet has on its shelves a now forgotten sex scandal, including an affair with a married man, her mentor in radio, and naked photos. Trump's name has graced companies gone bankrupt, he's flirted with it personally, and financial media including *Forbes* has doubted the size of his fortune. At this moment, quite a few investors in Trump-branded properties are upside down in huge losses. Dr. Phil's credentials are not much better than Dr. Brinkley's, but Tony has none—and has relied on a cheap carnival trick, the fire walk, as claim to fame. Still, my all-time favorite fact about a couple gurus is that Barbara DeAngelis, author of *Making Love Work*, and Dr. John Gray of *Men Are from Mars, Women from Venus* fame are divorced from each other—bitterly.

The point of all that? The marketplace pretty much accepts you as you position and present yourself, especially if you put yourself forward forcefully and aggressively enough, utilizing the time-tested and proven strategies of self-promotion.

# PRINCIPLE #8

## SELL TO PROPERLY PREPARED
# PROSPECTS

# 13

# Set The Stage for Success

*By Chip Kessler*

**B**ig-time entertainers have learned this important lesson very well over the years. You'll also notice it whenever you see and hear an important speaker. Few just walk out and go to work. Instead, anticipation is built, even some impatience created, and the stage is carefully set to support the star.

An example, go to any major music concert or comedy show and it's not the headliner that opens the show. Usually it's an up and coming act. Sometimes it's a former big name on the way down performing this role. Many entertainers now use elaborately produced video introductions before they take the stage in person. They are helped by expectations built by their other media exposure occurring and accumulating in advance of an audience seeing them perform in person. Famous comedians with a lot of television exposure like the Blue Collar Comedy gang benefit by audiences expecting them to be funny. Speakers learn the importance of a well-written introduction delivered by an enthusiastic endorser, as well as the harm that can be done by a poor introduction.

**Similarly, anyone selling anything can benefit from or be harmed by how the stage is set and what expectations are created before they perform**. Dr. Brinkley knew well that he was not making an easy sale. After all, the goat gland surgery that Brinkley was doing cost far more than the bottle of magic elixir he used to peddle on the medicine show stage. And the good doctor was wise enough to realize that even though his cure for male impotence was appealing to strong emotions, he wanted to do everything in his power to insure that all potential patients that visited him in Milford, Kansas were ready to seal the deal.

Prospective out-of-town patients making inquiries of the physician's services were sent carefully written sales letters complete with news of Brinkley's opening acts as they were. People such as bus driver "Happy Harry" and the doctor's wife Minnie were part of the form letter's "show". Over time, John Brinkley built out increasingly elaborate packages of literature placed in the hands of prospective patients before they came for consultation. **These materials had two tasks: one, to sell the appointment, and convince a prospective patient to engage in inconvenient, costly travel by train to the Brinkley Hospital. Two, to mentally and emotionally prepare the prospective patient to accept Dr. Brinkley's prescription as gospel to be trusted, and to accept the stiff fee as appropriate**. Then, when the would-be

**FROM THE BRINKLEY BLUEPRINT:**
*A thorough, thought-out process for preparing the prospect to buy—before a selling situation occurs or buying decision is asked for.*

patients were ready for the in-person consultation, they would travel to Milford via train and when arriving at the local depot, there was "Happy Harry" all decked out in his chauffeur's cap with a smile on his face ready to drive the newly arrived male-in-need to the Brinkley Clinic. Minnie played the role of official greeter when the bus pulled up to the clinic's door. Her smile and reassuring voice served as a means of saying, "you've made the right decision!"

It wasn't until the bus was unloaded and the patient(s) were ushered into the facility's special "meet and greet" room that Dr. John R. Brinkley in the flesh made his first appearance. It was time. As the public address announcer at the old Yankee Stadium would bellow out before the last of the ex-pinstripers emerged from the dugout and walked onto the field...

"Introducing the Greatest Yankee of them all,
The 'Yankee Clipper' Joe DiMaggio."

...the crowd would rise as one to its collective feet and proceed to give Joltin' Joe a welcome fit for such a high profile introduction.

Dr. John R. Brinkley for his day and time hit a lot of home runs too, not the least of which was how he first presented himself to a grateful crowd in his clinic, his personal Yankee Stadium if you will, because he was the one that could make these men feel like a superstar in the bedroom again. His prospective patient was thoroughly prepared, their arrival and his grand entrance perfectly choreographed. Is yours?

# 14

# Sale Delayed, Sale More Easily Made

*By Dan S. Kennedy*

**or many years, I've been utilizing an unusual, contrarian strategy, of deliberately delaying the selling**, in order to better prepare the prospect for buying. I have gotten a few clients to use it, but most frankly resist it and won't stick with it. I teach it, but I know most won't accept it. The idea is that selling to a poorly prepared prospect is a stressful struggle for salesperson and prospect alike, so the entire process can be significantly improved by deliberately delaying the sales presentation until elements critical to a prospect's readiness to buy can be put in place—such as trust, authority, category of one status, price or fee appropriateness.

For people with a 'sales instinct' or a great deal of traditional sales experience, or an urgent need for income, the tendency to leap on a prospect the first moment he reveals himself and sell, sell, sell is irresistible. Gotta get 'em before they get away.

**Long, long before I adopted the deliberately delayed sale strategy, John Brinkley employed it**, initially born more of logistics and necessity than of genius. In his case, most of his patients had to travel great distances, most by train, to visit his clinic. They weren't local patients who might see an advertisement today, call today, be eager for an appointment tomorrow, and be brought in for that appointment with no advance preparation, placing the entire burden of moving that person from very tentative interest to a commitment on the doctor. Dr. Brinkley wasn't able to make this mistake. Instead, the distance and inconvenient travel that stood between his patients and his clinic compelled him to develop a strategy for making a delayed sale. In our terminology today, he generated leads, then had to send media to those leads, putting the burden on it to move the prospect from tentative interest to the first commitment; costly travel for consultation; then, there, moving that prospect the rest of the way to complete commitment. Forced into this, Brinkley began with fairly simple sales letters, but graduated to what I now call a "shock 'n awe package". Those packages I build today are typically multi-media, including a sales letter, other printed literature, a book, audio CD, DVD, packaged in an impressive manner. Clients incur fees upwards from $50,000.00 to have me develop theirs, for very good reason; they can be "game-changers".

**My personal modus operandi has long been the delayed sale**, with some version of a shock 'n awe package delivered between the prospective client's query and the time I finally have a personal conversation with him. So, for example, when someone called my office to inquire about booking me to speak for their company's or association's meeting, I never—repeat: never—either immediately jumped on the phone to engage that prospect, or returned a call or had a phone appointment arranged before delivering a package of my material and allowing a few days for its review. Most of my peers who became aware of my approach were terrified by it and wouldn't dare use it, fearing the impatient prospect would simply move on to someone else and book them. I do not believe in conducting business fearfully. Consequently, I relied on this approach virtually from the very start of my career, even when I really needed the income from every sale, and certainly couldn't afford to lose any unnecessarily. Typically, by the way, I sent a package including copies of my books, one of my audio cassette products, a professional brochure, a stack of testimonials, and some articles, with as much of it as possible hand-picked to be relevant to the prospect, and often with pages Post-It Note® flagged for that prospect.

Clients of mine who have had shock 'n awe packages and delayed sale strategies developed for them, and had them proven superior to other strategies, include one of the top 100 real estate agents in the world, two major healthcare companies with clinics or offices nationwide, a financial planning firm, a major national insurance company (for the recruiting of agents), and several providers of franchise and non-franchise business development systems sold to doctors, lawyers, and other types of business owners. Interestingly, in those latter cases, they must convince interested prospects to travel across the country to a "discovery day" at their businesses, to there decide on and buy their program, much as John Brinkley needed his prospective patients to travel to his clinic before ever deciding to buy his procedure.

I am a big believer in this kind of 'setting the stage' before delivering any performance, whether sales presentation, consultation and diagnosis, speech or professional service. However, I think it is of greatest importance in selling situations where the hurdles the prospect must be helped over are, to him, quite high—perhaps price or significant time commitment or acceptance of something for which extreme skepticism or fear may exist. That might be commitment by a fearful patient to major dental treatment, a business owner to switching to an entirely new computer system, or, in my cases, risking putting me on stage in front of the client's employees or association members and incurring substantial expense in doing so, or hiring me to re-invent their advertising, at substantial expense. These are major commitments, as was the decision to permit goat glands surgery!

---

SPECIAL NOTE: My procedures for "Takeaway Selling"—which include deliberately delaying the sale—are explored in detail in my book *No B.S. Sales Success in the New Economy*. A very in-depth examination of Sales Choreography® can be found in Sydney Barrows' book *Uncensored Sales Strategies*, to which I contributed.

*Cover, page 3 (After 21 Years...), page 4 ("Silver Wedding"), and page 5 ("Are You Sick?") from the 52-page "Success Story" brochure, one of many marketing pieces developed by John Brinkley, used in what Dan Kennedy now calls a shock'n awe package. (The entire book is included along with other samples of Dr. Brinkley literature in the complete Home Study Course available at www.ChipKessler.com)*

## PRINCIPLE #9

GIVE REASONS TO BELIEVE,
TO PEOPLE WHO WANT TO
# BELIEVE

# 15

# Do You Have "What It Takes" To Compel Immediate Action?

### By Chip Kessler

**A**t core, what was **THE secret** that made John Brinkley's fame and fortune, his self-creation of the lifestyle of big money, fancy cars, mansions, larger than life vacations, and being able to build his own hospitals, buy his own radio stations, and amaze the nation, versus just eking out a living or having to find another line of work altogether? What ONE THING more than any other propelled Dr. Brinkley to the mountaintop?

**What ONE THING, more than any other**, enabled Brinkley to motivate men to spend large sums of money for a goat-gland transplant and travel hundreds of miles to a strange city to first meet with him, and then to *instantly* agree to get the operation? And to motivate these men's wives to support them in this decision? Think about this for a moment—after all, how many wives usually approve of their husbands spending large sums of money on anything? Indeed, Dr. Brinkley's emotionally charged marketing messages stirred something in both genders.

It is difficult to synthesize this Brinkley "power" into a simple explanation. After a great deal of thought, while pouring over thousands of pages of information about John Brinkley's amazing success, archives of his materials, recordings of his radio broadcasts, and other resources, I decided to put it this way: Dr. Brinkley did not merely advertise, market, promote, sell. He was a *motivational* personality. John R. Brinkley developed the ability to make people get the "desire to believe." Not just making them believe; that's cross between parlor tricks and classic salesmanship. The greater success is making people *want to* believe. This one element can move mountains in your business; no matter what business you are presently in or want to be in.

When was the last time that you made a decision or purchase, or took an action, and there was no doubt in your mind that you were making the right decision and moving forward on it? In your heart and mind, you knew what you were doing was right.

**JOHN R. BRINKLEY** *did* NOT *merely advertise, market, promote, sell. He was a* MOTIVATIONAL *personality.*

Dr. Brinkley had this effect on people, and it made him stand head and shoulders above the average run-of-the-mill marketer, anyone else offering any product, service or cure. Most importantly, John Brinkley found ways to connect to the most profound reasons someone would want to believe in him and his proposition.

A great example of this was handed to John Brinkley, but to his credit, he recognized its potential value when it occurred. John's gift came from that farmer who first went to the Milford, Kansas physician because he lacked "pep." John R. Brinkley's handy-work below the belt not only brought praises from the famer Bill Stittsworth and his wife (remember, she was so elated with her man's newly rediscovered sexual ability that she then wanted to have ovaries from a female goat transplanted herself), it also brought one other thing:

### Billy Stittsworth, *Jr.*

There are ways of letting your target market know about the effectiveness of what product and service you are marketing ... and then there are *ways*. The best is some evidence of the validity of your proposition that is intensely, profoundly motivational, triggering desire to believe. The emergence of a Stittsworth off-spring not only spoke volumes about the transformative power of Brinkley's goat-glands surgery, but also tapped into the greatest desire many men and women have: the need to have a baby. For the man, it's the continuation of his name. For the woman it coincides with her need to bring life into the world. In John Brinkley's time, it was still seen as the natural, expected fulfillment of marriage, and the absence of offspring represented embarrassing failure—a sign that, either the woman was barren or the man not a man at all. A couple without at least one child was not blessed by God, and family, friends, even the entire community wondered why, and viewed them with pity. These were the cultural conditions into which Dr. Brinkley had brought his cure. And now, Brinkley had an in-the-flesh demonstration of what a goat's transplanted testicles into a man can produce! The farmer's story and his living, breathing son provided a rock-solid foundation for others' belief.

**HIGH VALUE QUESTION:** *how do you... how can you inspire the desire to believe?*
*(Can you list ten ways you do this?)*

John Brinkley knew how to present his 'miracle' in a way that made people want to believe. Billy Jr. provided the unassailable reason to believe. This is a most potent combination. And Dr. Brinkley took full advantage, turning the farmer, his wife and little Billy Jr. into what we would now call 'compensated spokespersons', presenting them to groups of potential patients in person and through media at every opportunity.

**The million-dollar question then is**: how can you inspire the desire to believe, and what walking, talking, living, evidentiary demonstration can you present, providing unassailable reason to believe?

# Turning Your Persuasive Power Up From Half To Full With John Brinkley's Greatest Secret

### By Dan S. Kennedy

O ne of the most interesting personalities who I spent 'green room' time with, while a speaker 25+ times a year on the SUCCESS tour was the famous, buckskin-jacketed, silver-haired, homespun-talking criminal defense attorney, Gerry Spence. Spence said that it was damnably hard to gain acquittal even if all the facts were on the defendant's side *if the jury didn't want to believe*. Obviously, arguing on behalf of a client who the jury wanted to believe innocent, a huge advantage. I suppose that's not surprising, is it? We can assume that a major contributing factor to the Los Angeles jury's willingness to believe the police had planted evidence, willing to believe that the DNA evidence was contaminated, eager to believe "if it doesn't fit, you must acquit" was the inherent desire to believe O.J. innocent. I happen to be one of the few white guys walking around who has steadfastly maintained an open mind about O.J. Simpson being innocent of the murders, and I have to admit that I want to believe he is.

**What Chip has identified as the single most important factor in Dr. Brinkley's remarkable success—*the desire to believe*—is a little-understood, extremely powerful force that, when consciously and deliberately harnessed, can lift an ordinary man or women to great heights of influence, fame and fortune, and fuel the growth of a business as nothing else.**

Putting this force to work, as your ally should be a high priority. This force is at work in every aspect of life. What Eric Hoffer identified as 'the true believer' in his must-read book of that same title, is someone who arrives at a point where their desire to believe 'x' is so great they refuse to indulge in critical thinking about it, or to consider information or opinion in opposition to it. Devout followers of any religion refuse to objectively question it or acknowledge any of its incongruities. Victims of a financial fraud like Bernie Madoff's ignore even the most obvious signs of something amiss—in his case, uninterrupted, consistent, above par returns. Partisan political purists and ideologues will remain committed to a course of action or to a candidate or elected leader despite abundant evidence of failure. It is sadly common for repeatedly abused wives to excuse the abuse and accept one promise after another broken promise after another broken promise from the violent husband that "it will never happen again." Yes, there may be complex psychology at work in her staying in an abusive relationship, but a major factor is that she wants to believe. Again, putting this force to work, as your ally should be high priority!

I once got to know a very rich psychic. He performed a fairly ordinary stage act with superb style, and at its end, made it known that he occasionally accepted private clients for in-depth personal readings. From those, he picked off mostly rich widows, but sometimes CEO's, investors, and others, for whom he could somehow employ his psychic powers for perfectly moral and ethical profit making, and share in the profits. His impressive mansion high up Camelback Mountain in Scottsdale, Arizona was paid for by the royalties he received from oil wells drilled at sites he picked for an oil baron's widow. As he explained to me, he was picking the sites in a known oil field, and he selected many more dry holes than productive ones, and the premise itself—divining the existence of oil deep within the earth by psychic power—should be viewed with great skepticism, so why was he kept on retainer, and paid millions in royalties? Because she wanted to believe, and by several kinds of compelling demonstrations, he provided her with sufficient reason to believe.

The important 'secret' here to grasp is that providing reasons to believe is a rather ordinary, commonly understood exercise in persuasion, but it is "low power" unless and until it is paired with an inspired desire to believe.

In this chapter and the preceding one, Chip and I, and Dr. Brinkley, have revealed something to you of unmatched importance and value, if you will take the time to think about it at length, patiently, in search of opportunity to apply it to your business. If this book gets you seriously engaged in thinking about this specific subject, it will have earned its price ten-thousand fold.

# PRINCIPLE #10

# SPOTLIGHT

## EXTREMELY DRAMATIC SUCCESS EXAMPLES

# 17

# Others' Singing Your Praises

## By Chip Kessler

**D**r. John R. Brinkley didn't need to search too long for any number of wonderful and talented singers to fill up the hours on his radio stations that were devoted to this form of entertainment. The good doctor didn't have to look very far to have "ordinary folks" talk him up either when it came to his abilities as a physician and surgeon.

**The Brinkley marketing machine paid proper respect and reverence to the power of a well-crafted, heart-felt testimonial.** As introduced in our proceeding chapter, there was the real-life testimonial: little Billy Stittsworth, Jr., and his parents' enthusiasm, parents that only a short time earlier were looking at a life devoid of sex let alone offspring.

Could a marketer ask for a better testimonial in this situation than flesh and blood social proof? It's such a strong tool that today; social-proof is in the toolbox of every savvy marketer. Let's spend a few moments and offer up some "social proof" examples that have been paraded in front of us in all kinds of advertising:

- The plastic surgeon that uses before and after photos of a woman's nose, lips, eyes or figure. Common, almost, now essential. You may have heard my co-author, Dan Kennedy, talk about a one-time client of his, Dr. Robert Kotler, a cosmetic surgeon recently seen on the reality TV show Dr. 90210. When Dan was working with him, Dr. Kotler often held get-acquainted seminars for prospective patients and brought actual patients to the seminars… so, after showing their Before photos, people could see the After's in the flesh, ask them questions, and hear from them, not just about their successful surgeries, but about their lives… very much akin to Dr. Brinkley's bringing little Billy Jr. and his beaming parents in to meet groups of patients to-be at his clinic.

- The couple that was in deep debt and despair because they owed hundreds of thousands of dollars to the I.R.S. until they visited the expert tax attorney who arranged for them to pay "pennies on the dollar" in a settlement. We see them happily enjoying their beautiful home, maybe racing across the lake in their boat on a sunny day.

- The lonely man or woman who couldn't find love, until the online matchmaking service connected them with the perfect mate. We see them sitting close to each other on the couch, holding hands, smiling, as they speak of soul mates. We may see their wedding pictures. Their romantic walk on the beach.

Such social-proof testimonials can represent and speak only of reasons to believe. Under ideal circumstances, the savviest marketer presents those who can also motivate desire to believe.

I recall as a boy sending away for some information in the mid-1960's about a table-top dice pro football game. The game, for its day and time was rather expensive at $11.95 compared to other football games back then that were selling for $2.95 or $3.95. When the information arrived, it not only contained a full color brochure detailing every aspect of the game, how much fun it was to play, and how it was the next best thing to being a real pro football player yourself; the game company also sent along an eight and a half by fourteen inch sized piece of paper that contained one testimonial after another (on both sides of the page) from boys (full names along with cities and states) that had previously purchased the game, loved it, and had taken the time to write the company and tell them how much they loved it. I enjoyed reading those testimonials more than the game brochure because it made me picture myself playing the game and enjoying it as much as those guys that had written about it. I had a paper route at the time and you better believe that I started saving up my money to buy that game!

Customers are certainly not the only people you might want to have singing your praises. Depending on your business, you might want to have experts and credentialed authorities, local or national celebrities, professional peers, the media. But it's hard to trump the farmer and his wife, with little Billy Jr. in tow.

**In fact, a Brinkley strategy was to be alert for opportunities to capture *particularly dramatic* testimonials—something too few marketers focus deliberate effort on.** For that reason, Brinkley wasn't content to just treat the easy patients, such as younger men that could buck the odds of an unsuccessful goat gland transplant and still find their way back to sexual health because the onslaught of time hadn't yet taken its toll. An example cited in *Charlatan* recounts the "remarkable story of" 71 year old J.J. Tobias, a chancellor at the University of the Chicago School of Law. After going under the doctor's knife, Tobias is quoted as exclaiming how he felt "25 years younger … full of pep, strong, healthy … ready to go on with my work." Tobias goes on to tell how he was "ill, old and played out, but the operation has revived me." Brinkley was eager to operate on Tobias despite the low likelihood of the patient feeling he was improved because, if he did experience positive results, he would be an immensely valuable "poster boy". Not only was he 71 years old, but he was an influential leader at a respected academic institution. As it turned out, in his mind, J.J. Tobias went from old to new again, and he gladly sang the praises of the amazing Dr. Brinkley, including giving an interview that was published in the *Syracuse Herald* newspaper.

If you want to excel and stand out from competitors and clutter with social proof, it's not enough just to collect and present testimonials at random. To replicate Dr. Brinkley, you will seek and intentionally create and present exceptionally dramatic human interest stories from customers who not only provide reason to believe, but also motivate desire to believe.

# 18

# Extreme Measures

### By Dan S. Kennedy

Some years ago, I was involved in the marketing of a Home Study Course that guided 'virgins' into the mail-order business. The business was built around an individual with a true, dramatic rags-to-riches story rich with detail that made people want to believe. In short order, we had a number of good testimonials from different people, attesting to various degrees of success, to specific incomes, and to meaningful personal rewards—quitting dead-end jobs; being able to be stay-at-home moms; buying a vacation home, and the like. As one of our marketing tools, we had an audiocassette filled with these people telling their stories in their own words and their own voices. It was effective, but it was not the sort of one-of-a-kind, compelling demonstration that Dr. Brinkley had, with the farmer, wife and Billy Jr. or the 71-year-old J.J. Tobias or a number of other unique patients.

One day a cassette tape arrived at the office from a customer, entirely unsolicited. It was recorded imperfectly, with scratchy background and occasional clicks. On it, a young doctor identified himself and told of being in desperate financial circumstances when he had first answered our ad and obtained the information about our Course. He told of living in his car, homeless, and giving blood in order to get the money to buy the Course, and then to scrape together enough money to run his first tiny ads. He told of his doubt and anxiety, even feeling foolish trying our plan. Then he told of finding the first envelopes with cash orders in them in his Post Office box. He told of bootstrapping his business, quickly but methodically creating a growing income for himself, and soon moving from his car to an apartment, then to home. It's been some time and I no longer remember all the exact details. But at the time, my partner and I instantly knew what had arrived in that day's mail. Had I been familiar with the John Brinkley story then, I'd have said that our own little Billy Jr. had strolled in the door!

We immediately scrapped our existent audiotape and replaced it with this new one, and watched sales soar.

### *In Search Of Your Billy Jr.—and the courage to use him.*

I have not often received such a gift. But I have often worked hard at finding this sort of customer and extraordinarily dramatic story buried in a client's customer, client or patient constituency. I have gone looking. I have dug through dusty bins of correspondence, sent out surveys and letters, put people on phones calling hundreds and hundreds of customers, gone to great extremes in search of the equal of the homeless-man-who-gave-blood-to-buy-the-Course-that-made-him-a-millionaire or the impotent-farmer-and-disappointed-wife-transformed.

These days, there is a tougher regulatory environment than ever before, governing the presentation of extraordinary, dramatic customer testimonials, and it's necessary to be aware of all the legal limitations, and ramifications of pushing the limits. However, there remains a very clear path to legally and safely using these kinds of stories.

And you need not necessarily wait for them to come to you. One of the "greats" of the advertising field I made a point of studying when I began my career in that field was David Ogilvy, a fry-cook and door to door salesman who built the largest ad agency in the world from scratch, and became a legendary figure. Early on, Ogilvy made a "hit list" of marquee clients he wanted, not just because they would be valuable clients, but also because having them would distinguish him, attract attention, and create demand. He believed in the principle of attachment I mentioned earlier in this book, and made a conscious, deliberate point of striving to attach himself to clients that would elevate him in the eyes of the business community. As time went on, he deliberately pursued clients and then created advertising for them that he believed would yield extraordinary cocktail party stories and further his legend. I credit Ogilvy with my habit of seeking, and being very alert for what I call 'cache clients'. Whenever presented with the slightest opportunity, I have gone to extremes to get in those doors, and clients I've had like Weight Watchers International, Guthy-Renker, and Joan Rivers were obtained through relatively circuitous paths, with, for me, extraordinary effort.

**John Brinkley understood how valuable it was to be surrounded by a cast of characters with extremely dramatic stories to tell and a willingness to tell them.** He went to extremes, took risks (such as operating on a 71 year old man in poor health), and was forever vigilant for opportunities to create or embrace patients that would grow his legend.

**I second Chip's observation that most business owners and marketers do not place high enough value on these assets, and do not invest enough thought, time, money, energy and effort in finding or creating them.** To that end, I have a story from my earliest years in business:

I was a fledgling Amway distributor, a business from which I learned a great deal during my few years of involvement. I witnessed a high-level Distributor in my upline do something stunningly brilliant. A high school senior had a terrible accident that made the TV news and was written up in newspapers; he was working out in the gym on the trampoline, landed awkwardly, and broke his back, severed his spinal cord, winding up paralyzed. There was mention in the article of his concern over how he would be able to earn a living and support himself. This high-level Distributor made a point of getting to this young man and his family, paying to get their home wheelchair equipped and assisting with the expenses of in-home care, and then teaching the young man to become a telemarketer, selling Amway products. He worked closely with the fellow, day in, day out, investing untold hours, and did help the man establish a successful business with hundreds of retail customers. The story of the man's success was the subject of a feature story in the Cleveland newspaper. The man attended the leading distributor's monthly rallies, and served as a living, breathing, dramatic and unassailable reason to believe and—it did not need said, if *he* can succeed, what excuse could you possibly have for being a quitter? Whatever override compensation the high-level distributor received as this young man's sponsor was, I'm confident, trivial compared to the income he was able to create thanks to the young man's story and example.

There are two things you shouldn't miss. Any number of other multi-level marketing leaders, insurance brokers, real estate brokers, etc. could have done what this distributor did; gotten to the young man and his family, created an opportunity for him in their business, assisted him, mentored him, and acquired a Brinkley-style living, breathing example of examples of enormous value. *None did.* Second, this high-level distributor went to great extremes to make this happen. He recognized the potential value and invested appropriately.

The more I've learned about John Brinkley, the more impressed I've become with his ability to see the opportunity and value in people passing through his business life, and his willingness to go to extremes to separate them from all the others, and use them—if you wish, exploit them—to extraordinary extent.

There are always reasons for extreme success. I've always liked the book title and line used by a fellow I produced a TV infomercial with, a hypnotherapist, Dr. John Kappas, actress Florence Henderson's husband. John said, simply: no success is an accident. Why did John Brinkley rise to unparalleled fame and grandiose wealth, while countless other physicians of his time—fraudsters and charlatans of his ilk, and more legitimate innovators with groundbreaking treatments that worked—work their entire lives in oblivion, just earning a living? Of course, many never had Brinkley's ambition. Many would simply never dare to "go big" as Brinkley did. But never doubt there were many who thought about it, saw him and envied him, and bitterly resented his success when they knew they were the better doctors. This never changes. So why? What really propelled Brinkley? To borrow from John Kappas, extreme success is never an accident. It is almost always the product of going to extremes in everything combining for that success.

## PRINCIPLE #11

# AUDACITY
## AND THE BIG IDEA
## AND BIG PROMISE

# ⑲

# The Power of Audacity

*By Chip Kessler*

In a given 24 hours, we are constantly bombarded with images and messages. Today's consumer is connected to some media nearly every waking moment. This makes getting noticed; getting attention harder than ever, and being remembered a 'mission impossible.' John Brinkley didn't face as much competition for attention, but then it is relative. He certainly took the challenge seriously. However, he had a powerful advantage, too. The act of taking testicles from a male goat and transplanting them into a human male was a dynamic attention-getter! The subject matter was controversial … and Brinkley was quick to milk it for all it was worth. He didn't stop with talking about his current surgical procedure; he claimed that his success with goat glands transplants to restore sexual vitality and slow aging would soon lead to additional surgical advancements such as:

- ➤ Making blind people see via transplanting of goats' eyes
- ➤ Transplanting vital goats' organs so that the dead may live again

No documentation exists that the doctor ever attempted such medical procedures, but the sheer boldness of the statements brought the desired publicity and made the general public stand up and take even greater notice of John R. Brinkley.

**So here's a question for you**: have you been able to successfully tap into the "Power of Audacity" for your marketing message?

Barack Obama got to the White House talking about the audacity of hope, and he had the audacity to run for the presidency with, arguably, less experience than any other serious candidate, in a primary contest against "the Clinton machine", ultimately to become America's first black President. Whatever you think of his ideology, politics, or performance as President, you have to admire the improbable achievement of getting the keys to 1600 Pennsylvania Avenue. How did this happen? There are certainly similarities between his campaign and campaign style and that of John Brinkley's campaign for the hearts and minds of his patients, and for public acclaim. They both used the newest media of their time creatively and aggressively. The Obama campaign staged elaborately produced events more akin to rock concerts than traditional campaign rallies—and even had women in the audience swooning and fainting. The campaign also made extensive use of the Internet and its social media. John Brinkley delivered impassioned monologues on the radio, staged dramatic events for the media including permitting viewing of his actual surgeries on several occasions, and utilized live, walking, talking testimonials as no doctor had ever before imagined doing. Brinkley's promise was obviously audacious. So were Obama's.

Dan Kennedy points out that there are now so many choices of goods, services, experiences and providers in every category that few will tolerate let alone be interested in anything that seems ordinary. His associate, Bill Glazer, wrote an entire book about "outrageous advertising." There is now a pressing need to adopt the Brinkley blueprint in this regard: having the audacity to bring a bigger than life, bolder than ever before made USP (Unique Selling Proposition) forward as your own.

We're back to that word again, audacity. With its power there is hazard. It's one thing to make all kinds of outrageous claims, promises or guarantees; quite another to be able to back them up. This requires any marketer concerned with long-term customer value and with the law to walk a fine line between fiction and reality, something John R. Brinkley's critics believed he crossed with abandon. Countless marketers continue to walk on the wild side today, such as the fortune teller/psychic who claims to be able to tell you the future, or in a more conventional sense, the financial guru/money wizard who says he knows how to turn your small nest egg into a giant sized nest large enough to house five fully grown eagles, six large owls and nine full-sized ostriches through winning stock market tips, made with his secret formula. While you may shake your head at the idea of selling such an audacious proposition, I invite you to check the pages of *Investor's Business Daily* this very week. You will find at least one full-page advertiser insisting he, in fact, has some secret, proprietary, magic formula for making money 100% of the time regardless of market ups and downs.

**In short, audacity is advantage.**

For the individual making audacious promises, a carefully cultivated and promoted Dynamic Persona is important. The stock market guru isn't driving around in a ten year old clunker but rather is seen in a Bentley, Rolls Royce, or perhaps a Ferrari. He may present himself as a man of great controversy, at odds with the Wall Street establishment. Or as a man of science, who has brought a unique discipline to investing, based not on traditional financial thought, but on nuclear physics. Or as a confidante of the rich, famous and mighty, photographed with Hollywood, sports and business celebrities. One way or another, he will create an aura of intrigue and interest for himself—he will never be personally unimportant, with all the focus directed at his product.

**Likewise, John R. Brinkley was careful to cultivate such an aura.** He told the world that he was a serious and driven student of his craft. Brinkley presented himself as a cloistered man, someone not easily available just because someone wanted to speak with him, even a potential patient. In his radio broadcasts, he made it forcefully clear that he did not accept just anybody as a patient, and had to be convinced of your sincerity. He did not run from the fact that he was at odds with the medical establishment; he made much of his rogue status. He told of other doctors' and hospitals' failures and of his dramatic life-saving successes. He made himself big and important—he did not just have an office or clinic; he had The Brinkley Hospital. Once achieved, he also made no secret of his success and wealth, displaying exotic luxury automobiles, mansions and a lifestyle of the rich and famous.

**Brinkley wanted people thinking *about him*.** He wanted people wondering what he was up to in his efforts to perfect his surgical techniques. He wanted people believing he was engrossed in the scientific world and its potential for new discoveries. In Brinkley's mind, the less accessible he made himself, the more people would look at him as someone they wanted to know more about. The stronger a position he took against "the establishment", the more people would trust him and turn to him when disappointed with the ordinary measures of care they received from their family physician or local hospital. The more audacious and outrageous his stories of medical miracles, the more he would be believed—a way of thinking foreign to many, on its surface irrational, yet genius in its understanding of the human psyche. In short, Brinkley wanted there to be a 'legend of John Brinkley' spread far and wide. Even his most eccentric and outlandish personal behavior fed that legend. At different times, he performed as a six-gun shooter and quick draw artist at public events; he ran afoul of the law, notably including an incident when he got drunk and hacked up a neighbor's automobile with an axe; he was seen chasing someone from his hospital, wielding a knife. He was infamous for his hot temper. According to the author of *Charlatan*, people just chalked it all up to the amazing doctor's genius, because those of his extraordinary intelligence, who worked under such intense pressure, had to let off some steam every once and awhile! Beyond audacious behavior, but accepted behavior thanks to the Brinkley mystique which he had deliberately created. To sum it up:

## Audacity + Curiosity + Respect = MONEY

Deep down, most people admire the bold and daring, and even the dysfunctional if associated with genius. (Think of the years that Michael Jackson's outrageous and odd excesses—like building an amusement park and stocking a zoo at his home—built his legend and heightened fans' curiosity about him, and think of the many people who overlooked, acted as apologists for, and excused his most bizarre behavior.) Brinkley dared to step out from the crowd in his words, his actions, and his persona. The result was a national fascination with him that poured millions into his coffers.

# ⟨20⟩

# The Sources of Power

*By Dan S. Kennedy*

I worked for a time very closely with a man who had so much in common with John Brinkley, when I listened to the Brinkley radio broadcasts, I could easily imagine my friend giving them, in exactly the same style and tone. My friend did not sell health; he sold wealth, but otherwise, they might have been twins. And I watched firsthand as he started with but a few people attracted to him through advertising and rapidly multiplied them, converting them to zealous missionaries, having them spread his legend far and wide, so that in short order, there were thousands and then tens of thousands of followers, and huge sums of money flowing in—some of which bought all manner of media, to pour even more gasoline on the fire. I witnessed this phenomenon of phenomena firsthand, and as a result, can see in my imagination John Brinkley's progress week by week.

I can definitely tell you what the sources of all the power were in the drama that I witnessed and to some extent, was a part of. Those, the very same sources of the power that brought Brinkley up from small-time, magic elixir hustler to the most famous (and then infamous) medical man of his time.

They are simple to cite, but, frankly, relatively few entrepreneurs, marketers, authors or others have the brass balls and, arguably, recklessness, or to use Chip's chosen term, the unbridled audacity to use the 'secrets' even when understood. Whether you do or not, I obviously can't predict.

**The power is in proportion to the bigness, the grandiosity, and the extreme audacity of The Idea and of The Promise.**

There has to be a single Big Idea on which the brightest possible spotlight shines. You might summarize Brinkley's as: *youth restored*. We did summarize my friend's as: you—yes, *you*—a millionaire? (And, in the late 1970's and early 1980's, "millionaire" meant something much more profound than it does today.) Personally, incidentally, I fueled the making of a small fortune with a single Big Idea for its intended audiences: Magnetic Marketing®. That meant and was explained as: easy attraction rather than difficult pursuit, so for salespeople it meant an immediate and permanent end to ugly, unpleasant prospecting; to small business owners, an end to waste of money on unproductive advertising, an end to worry about where the next customer might come from. If you stop and think about Brinkley's choice of Big Idea, you can certainly argue it was a better choice than mine. Consider just how many things are bought and how much money is spent on the relatively futile, and with passing years, increasingly desperate pursuit of youth restored. I can show you two very expensive classic cars in my garages that are testament.

Maybe the greatest, most amazing marketing and promotional feat ever accomplished is Christianity. Reportedly, by one guy, starting with but a handful of followers. With a very Big Idea: salvation and eternal

life after death in the kingdom of heaven.
Is there anything people fear more, deep
down, than the end?

**FROM THE
BRINKLEY
BLUEPRINT:**
*1. THE Big Idea
2. THE Big Promise*

The bigger and bolder The Big Idea,
the more powerful. The more connected
to deeper meanings and deeply held emotions—fears and desires—the
better. What most marketers think of as a Big Idea is actually quite small.

## *A Big Idea Can Command Attention, But It Takes A Big Promise To Fuel A Movement Or A Fortune*

I don't claim to be a theologian, but it seems to me you can boil
Christianity's Big Promise down to this: *believe—and you're in.* There's
a secular version of this, by the way, originally imported here from
England; popularized, ironically, by a minister, Dr. Norman Vincent
Peale; at the heart of "the success-thought movement" from beginning
to present. It fueled Napoleon Hill's career in the 1940's; it fueled Tony
Robbins' career more recently. A few years ago, all eyes focused on the
video 'documentary' titled *The Secret*. Its "stars" appeared everywhere,
from Oprah to Larry King to *TIME* and *Newsweek*. The Big Promise of
it all: think a certain way i.e. believe, and whatever you desire will come
to you. This is a very big and extremely appealing promise principally
because of all it omits—like, say, *and work*.

I am and have long been a serious student of marketing, and
particularly of extraordinary, extreme marketing successes, be they
companies or products or individuals, be they legitimate or daring frauds
or something inhabiting the gray territories in between. I look at each, to

identify The Big Idea and The Big Promise. This is endlessly fascinating to me, and it has aided me in creating my own little legend and my own small fortune, and aided me in my work for my clients. I would encourage you to engage in this same analysis, and more importantly, to identify your own Big Idea and Big Promise, and to assess just how big or small they really are.

## PRINCIPLE #12

# MAKING
### PRICE OF NO IMPORTANCE

# 21

# Prescription for Unlimited Price Elasticity

*By Chip Kessler*

**M**y co-author Dan Kennedy ranks Price as one of the most interesting aspects of marketing, and says that he has probably helped more people make more money with price strategies than with any other type of strategies. From him, that's a very big endorsement for the importance of price. I understand he's at work on an entire book on the subject. One of Dan's favorite concepts is: price elasticity—that most people could be successfully stretching their prices higher, and that there can be conditions created that make a price otherwise thought of as too high or unaffordable, acceptable.

**Dr. John R. Brinkley understood the importance of price—and price elasticity—very well.** He sold at far above par, premium prices, and paying the doctor his fees was a very big stretch of mind-set and budget, even a great hardship for many of his patients—not to mention the fact that most had to take days away from farm, business or job, and travel great distance by train to arrive at Dr. Brinkley's hospitals. In his time, the size of the fees Dr. Brinkley demanded was breathtaking. As audacious as was his marketing.

You might be quick to insist that the good doctor was in a unique position because of the unique nature of what he was offering to the sexually downtrodden man. You might even say that he had advantage of fraudulent promise that you do not have and would not want. True enough, but there's no profit to be found in such excuses. The opportunity for gain lies in somehow finding or creating the basis for placing yourself in the same extremely advantageous position in the marketplace and in the public mind that Dr. Brinkley took for himself. The opportunity is in making yourself and your proposition of the same kind of unique importance as Dr. Brinkley and his proposition. That is the key to having whatever price you may ask eagerly and willingly paid, even by customers who are at first stunned by it, and even by customers who must struggle to pay it (if you choose to sell to such customers).

There were three things that made it possible for John Brinkley to command the extraordinarily high fees that he did, from a virtually unlimited number of patients, with virtually no resistance, and all three are replicatable.

First, it must be noted that Dr. Brinkley's patients rarely questioned how his goat gland transplant surgery actually worked. There was a pre-supposition that goats were sexual dynamos, well known by people at the time, as most were farmers or lived among farmers. In fact, it's thought that that first farmer who came to Brinkley in search of solution for his "lack of pep" and sexual dysfunction may have suggested the goat glands transplant to Brinkley, rather than the other way around. Brinkley built on **an existent foundation of accepted fact.**

This is extremely important. The sale of countless "Hollywood secrets" for losing weight quickly, for ageless beauty, is possible because of an existent foundation; that actors and actresses possess such secrets is accepted fact for

**FROM THE BRINKLEY BLUEPRINT:** *Building on the existent foundation of accepted fact.*

many people. Similarly, stock-pickers' tips are sold because its accepted fact that Wall Street insiders have privileged (and possibly illegal) access to information the rank and file investor does not. Tips of which horses to bet (in Dan Kennedy's world) or which sports teams to wager on are sold by purported insiders playing up their connections to this same accepted fact. The entire industry of 'how to get rich in real estate' and its audacious claims of being able to do so with no money or credit and little training, nearly overnight, was based on an existent foundation of accepted fact—until recently, there was broad public acceptance of real estate as a good investment vehicle. If you are not reminding your prospective customers of the existent foundation of accepted fact that supports your proposition, you are missing out on something important.

Because there was no question about the validity of Dr. Brinkley's process, he avoided being in a defensive position about its price.

## *The All-Time, Best-Ever Answer To Price*

Second, Dr. Brinkley was a legend, famous as a brilliant, innovative, dedicated healer and physician sought out by people from great distances away. The answer to price was implicit: *because it's Dr. Brinkley, that's why.* The price might be seriously questioned if put forward by someone else.

This is true of any number of individuals and professionals, as well as luxury brand companies and their products. If, upon citing your prices or fees to a family member or friend who questions them, your customer doesn't automatically give the 'because it's Dr. Brinkley, that's why' answer, you are failing to put something important in place.

Third, Dr. Brinkley made use of the influence of supply and demand. There was, after all, only one Dr. Brinkley, and he could perform only a limited number of operations. He made it clear that there were more people vying for his attention and assistance, with this operation, and with other health matters, than he had attention to give. He further made it clear that he was somewhat arbitrary in choosing who would be accepted and who would be turned away, so you needed to follow his instructions precisely, to the letter; convince him of your sincerity; and avoid offending or annoying him. In such an environment, who would dare question fees?

Ultimately, Dr. Brinkley even discovered differential pricing, to offer a premium-priced service to an affluent few. To the prospective Brinkley surgical candidate who revealed he could pay for the very best, Dr. Brinkley offered this suggestion: why lower yourself to receiving what the common ordinary man receives in the form of testicles from a goat when you can have implanted in your body the glands from a healthy young man!

Here, Brinkley was more than willing to offer the man of means the rare opportunity to have something that not every prospective patient had the wherewithal to obtain, and his marketing message made this perfectly clear. The doctor allowed that he was privy to getting human male testicles and that naturally such an item was pricier. Why wouldn't it be, Brinkley reasoned since goat glands are from a goat and male testicles are from a man!

Presumably, you won't be offering a choice between goat glands and a virile young man's private parts. But you can still follow the Brinkley blueprint behind this astounding proposition: extreme, dramatic difference between the product or service you sell to the majority of your customers and a much higher priced, exclusive, very limited in supply alternate version of that product or service offered to a discerning few, for whom price is no object in securing the best, and securing what others cannot have.

# PRINCIPLE #13

## CAPITALIZING ON
# ELITISM

# 22

# What Others Cannot Have

*By Chip Kessler*

**D**onald Trump's right-hand man, George Ross, who spoke at one of the Glazer-Kennedy Insider's Circle™ yearly Marketing and Moneymaking SuperConferences, makes the profound point: *there's never any trouble selling the penthouse*—especially when it consumes the entire top floor of the building.

Given that such a penthouse may command a million dollars more than the identically sized home one floor below, why would such a statement hold true in the business of high-rise condominiums? Of course. There is only one penthouse. Only one person can possess it and in doing so, he possesses what many others wanted and want but were too late to acquire, or cannot afford, and cannot have. This desire for what others cannot have can be found at work in countless other fields and selling situations, and fortunes made, if you look.

Referring back to the previous Chapter, I made mention of Dr. Brinkley's invention of his own penthouse to sell transplants of human testicles instead of goat glands. If you thought the goat gland transplants were way out there, imagine the medical establishment's reaction to this! Such objections and legalities and ethics notwithstanding, the significant business principle is that John Brinkley recognized that, within the flow of customers coming to him, there were some who would gladly pay an even higher fee in order to possess something that the masses could not have.

In Dr. Brinkley's own words, in defense of this procedure, and in presenting it to candidates:

1. The client was able to afford such luxury so <u>why should he *settle* for less</u> than the best?

2. Such human glands were certainly <u>not easy to get</u> but Dr. Brinkley had his proprietary sources

3. These were no ordinary human glands, but those of a healthy, virile young male

4. Did the patient really want the glands *from a goat* transplanted inside his body? (Yes, Brinkley was willing and bold enough to sell against his own product!)

5. Because human glands are not always accessible, the patient must be ready at a moment's notice to make himself available for the surgery

6. This procedure using the human glands <u>was so superior and reliable that a performance/satisfaction guarantee could be made</u>—unheard of, of course, in medicine: a guarantee that the

human glands will be of the highest quality and if there is any dissatisfaction then they patient may request a new set free-of-charge (only having to pay basic hospital costs)

Now let's examine these price justification marketing points:

1.  Appealing to one's sense of ego and pride because you obviously are a man that appreciates the finer things in life and you have the intelligence and means to get what you want

2.  Promoting the fact that not everyone who wants a set of human glands can get them but because you have had the good fortune to learn about Dr. John R. Brinkley, the only man around who can procure such a precious commodity, and are a discerning and accomplished and therefore affluent individual, you can

3.  Highlighting the exclusive nature of what the patient will receive, as in "young" and "healthy." Also enticing the prospect with the knowledge that the words "young" and "healthy" in this context imply sexual stamina and increased sexual ability and pleasure.

4.  An additional ego appeal: you're a human male so why sink to the level of implanting something from a goat inside your body, especially in this most important region of your being? As well, talking up the medical/health aspects of goat versus human testicles being transplanted inside you. (Keep in mind that only a select few amongst the doctor's prospective patients ever got to learn about the availability of human testicles. The majority of men were only aware that Dr. Brinkley was offering to make them whole again via a goat's virility.)

5.  Conveying excitement into the mix as in "you'll not know when this special gift will arrive so I'll need you standing by; ready to jump when I call." The prospective patient lies in bed at night wondering if tomorrow will be the day!

6.  Taking away any fear or concern of failure. Brinkley took away the last vestige of doubt, with a guarantee.

It is really no secret that the affluent want what others cannot have. They prefer living in gated enclaves; they invest in original art and rare collectibles; they want to attend sporting events in their own luxury skyboxes or at least ringside seats; they eschew first class commercial air travel in favor of private jets; they join private clubs; and vie to get their offspring admitted to elite, private pre-schools, academies and universities. This is motivation clearly seen at work in almost all the buying behavior of the rich. But it lives in the minds of the less affluent too, regardless of their ability or inability to indulge it. "Keeping up with Joneses" may drive much of the Chevrolet crowd's purchasing, but a desire to get one up on the Joneses is ever-present, and can be used by astute marketers with just about any demographic group.

# 23

# Know Thy Customer. He's Probably An Elitist In His Heart.

## By Dan S. Kennedy

**A**s Chip pointed out, price strategies are a particular fascination of mine, and I view them as part of marketing—not mathematics, not formulaic by industry standards, and definitely not left to bean counters to calculate and set in place.

The preceding two Chapters demonstrate that John Brinkley viewed the matters of professional fees in much the same way. These Chapters display his cleverness, in protecting his prices from question, pre-empting fee resistance, and ultimately, advancing to different prices for different customers, a sophisticated opportunity missed by most businesspeople.

While I was working on this book, I brought a big portion of our family to Disney, Florida for a quick vacation. There was a time when the experience at the Disney parks was entirely democratic, meaning there was one price paid by all, and everybody stood in the same lines, potentially waiting the same length of time in blazing sun, oppressive humidity, or even thunderstorms. To get a photo of their child with a Disney character, everybody hurried to a spot and took their place in line and waited, right along with everybody else. Prince or pauper, same line, same wait, same experience. This began to change some time ago, and the pace and breadth of the change seems to be accelerating. First innovation: the Speed-Pass, to be purchased, pretty much by all who would—which effectively divided Park customers roughly 1/3$^{rd}$ have's, 2/3rds have-not's. Next came the VIP Guides, presently at $195 an hour. Next, the Premium VIP Guides, at $295.00 an hour, 6 hour minimum... and there are a limited number of these. There are lines to wait in, for photos with characters, but there are also closed-door breakfasts and dinners with characters, for a fee. There are privileges only for guests staying at on-property Disney resorts, and different, better privileges only for guests staying on the concierge-floors of those resorts, benefits for stockholders, and benefits for Disney Vacation Club time-share owners. Democracy has yielded to tiered, hierarchal elitism at the Happiest Place on Earth.

Whether Walt would approve or not, I'm not sure, but *I* approve. Like the accomplished, affluent fellow to whom Dr. Brinkley quietly offered the superior option of human glands that few could have versus goat glands all could have, I prefer the best option available to me in many things, and I am an unapologetic elitist. I worked hard and continue to work hard in exchange for opportunities, rights, privileges, benefits, privacy, and luxury that others cannot have, and I'll admit that some of my enjoyment is fact that others can't have it.

We own a penthouse condo near Washington DC, chosen for practical reasons i.e. no noisy, furniture-moving, ballroom dancing neighbors above us, better resale value—but part of the pleasure of owning it is punching that top button and taking the elevator to the top, where others can't live. At Disney, we hired the $295 an hour guide for a number of practical reasons, but one of the family members accompanying me, embarrassed by the elitism of it, still quietly admitted that "the best ride of all is walking right past these long lines of tired, waiting people and immediately getting to the front". The looks on the faces of those stuck in those lines tell the story, but their envy can be *felt* even without looking.

If you are not motivated by this, one of three things is true: you are not affluent. Two, you aren't willing to admit it, and may not be conscious about why you buy what you buy, at what price, with what perceived or actual exclusivity. Three, you're a saint. There aren't many saints. My friend Glenn W. Turner, who created Koscot, a myriad of other 'Cot' companies including Minkcot, and Dare to Be Great, says that many women will tell you they don't want a mink coat—*where would they wear it? It's so showy and ostentatious!*—But it's dangerous to have any woman try one on in front of a mirror.

Dr. Brinkley primarily promoted himself to and spoke to, and spoke the language of, Everyman. The best direct-response copywriter I've ever studied and known, Gary Halbert, brilliantly spoke to Everyman this same way, with such genius

RESOURCES

*Book: No B.S. Marketing to the Affluent by Dan S. Kennedy*

Available at all booksellers, information at www.NoBSBooks.com

*Newsletter: No B.S. Marketing to the Affluent Letter*

Available at DanKennedy.com

and effectiveness, no other copywriter could top his results in head to head competition, if marketing to Everyman. The aforementioned Glenn Turner could inflame the passions and garner the trust of Everyman like no other speaker and pitchman I have ever known, observed or studied. But John Brinkley was also astute enough to realize that there's an elitist inside every man, and more important from a profit standpoint, every population attracted by a broad message includes some ultra-elitists not only eager but financially able to indulge their elitism, and he was able to speak persuasively to them as well.

# PRINCIPLE #14

## MAKING NEWS—BEING
# NEWS

# "Look. Up in the sky. It's Superman!"

### By Chip Kessler

**C**ommon sense says the more people that know you, the more comfortable they'll be in doing business with you. Remembering that perception is reality, people who *feel* they know you are just as comfortable buying from you as those who actually know you—perhaps even more so, as those who only feel they know you thanks to your deliberately crafted persona and promotion hold an idealized character and relationship in their minds that just might be better than the real thing!

Conversely, it's harder to feel at ease handing money over to a stranger. After all, your mother cautioned you against strangers, didn't she?

Dr. John R. Brinkley wisely set out to have the entire population of potential patients know of him, and, more importantly, feel that they knew him, and believe he was their friend and ally. His every foray into the media was with this central objective. He also recognized that what

139

others said about him was more powerful than what he might say, and that having others call peoples' attention to him was more influential than calling attention to himself. This conviction drove strategies like having books written about him, by others, which was highlighted earlier in this book. While Brinkley heavily invested in advertising, and in owning media outlets rather than just using them, he leveraged that into publicity, and used the power of publicity at every opportunity. His self-made prominence, his visibility from bought and paid for advertising, his far-outside-mainstream promise and surgical procedure, even the controversy that developed around him served him well in bringing reporters, journalists, and broadcasters to his door, eager to report on his story—whether as a modern marvel in medicine, or as an epic fraud. Journalists wanted to interview him, his associates and his patients. The result was more free ink than he could ever have afforded as paid advertising, with more impact. This kind of publicity is one of the rare instances when free is more valuable than paid.

As analogy, Superman never had to buy advertisements to announce his presence or call attention to his adventures or feats. The media was eager to report on him, and the public happily pointed up and yelled to all who might hear them: "Look, up in the sky—it's Superman!" Of course I know that Superman is a fictional hero, a product of imagination. But the principle is the point: getting people telling others of your legend is far more valuable than the telling of it yourself. And you don't have to put on a colorful costume and cape and leap over tall buildings in a single bound or stop a speeding locomotive with the extended palm of your hand. You only need an intriguing story, a dynamic persona, and visibility. Publicity will follow.

Take the late Dave Thomas for example. The owner of the Wendy's Restaurant business wisely decided to feature himself in his television commercials. Mr. Thomas would appear on your screen in 30-second spots for week upon week. He became both a familiar and welcome presence. People felt like they knew the man, and they liked him; he certainly seemed likeable.

How often have you said of some celebrity you've never actually met, "He's a nice guy", or at least "He seems like a nice guy"? Most of us have these feelings for a number of celebrities we've seen a lot of, grown up with, and developed fondness for. It's an illusion, of course, but an important one.

The television commercials brought to light the "Dave Thomas Story" and the fact that he'd been adopted. Interviews followed in newspapers, magazines and on radio and television. The media wanted to know all about this orphan/business owner/television personality. The publicity fed upon itself like a snowball rolling downhill. The end result: more Wendy's hamburgers, cheeseburgers, fries, chili and drinks were sold. And to Dave Thomas, that was the most important thing. In fact, nice guy image aside, going all the way back to Dave's first fast food venture, as owner of Kentucky Fried Chicken franchises, his close associates recall his unrestrained glee at driving local, independent competitors out of business, and remarking how much he enjoyed the sight of their boarded up storefronts.

Anyway, just as Dave Thomas used an intriguing personal story to sell burgers, Dr. Brinkley was adept at capturing or creating and using publicity-friendly human-interest stories to grow his legend and compel the media to gift him with free promotion.

## *Have Knife and Goat Glands—Will Travel!*

An excellent and instructive example is the doctor's venture into California, circa 1922. Harry Chandler, owner of the *Los Angeles Times* newspaper had challenged John R. Brinkley to come to the Golden State and prove both his mettle as a surgeon and the functionality of his claims. Brinkley's Kansas exploits with a knife had begun to draw attention far and wide, but for Chandler it was a matter of wanting to see for things himself and not taking any word-of-mouth marketing ploys from thousands of miles away. The skeptical publisher thought Brinkley might be getting away with pulling the wool over the eyes of rube farmers in the heartland, and might be exposed by the more sophisticated citizens of California. The shrewd publisher saw a great story, either way.

Chandler's challenge to Brinkley was quite simple: perform a goat gland transplant on one of his editors and if the results were as advertised, the newspaper mogul would let the entire state of California and even the nation know that the fountain of sexual youth and vitality really did exist ... and if the surgery failed then the full weight of the *Los Angeles Times* would come down on Brinkley, more than likely putting an end to the fraud once and for all.

Never one to back away from a marketing opportunity, the good doctor agreed. As author Pope Brock reports in *Charlatan:*

> *"... he first [Brinkley] operated on managing editor Harry E. Andrews. Success was proclaimed on March 23, 1922. Then the doctor did the same for a U.S. Circuit Court Judge, unnamed Hollywood screen stars, and others. According to several reports, Chandler received goat glands himself."*

The headline in the April 22, 1922 *Los Angeles Times* appeared as follows:

NEW LIFE IN GLANDS- DR. BRINKLEY'S PATIENTS HERE SHOW IMPROVEMENT- MANY VICTIMS OF "INCURABLE" DISEASES ARE CURED- TWELVE HUNDRED OPERATIONS ARE ALL SUCCESSFUL

In addition to making a tidy sum of money on the additional surgeries, Brinkley was the beneficiary of Harry Chandler's repeated praise. The publicity was so persuasive that one of the preeminent film comedians of the time, Buster Keaton inserted references about "goat-gland transplants" into his new feature motion picture, *Cops*.

The "challenge strategy" for securing publicity has had a long history, beyond John Brinkley. In the same era, Houdini made himself famous by visiting police stations and daring the constabulary to handcuff, chain, and imprison him so that he could not escape—and alerting the local media of the event. Decades after John Brinkley won over the prestigious and influential *Los Angeles Times*, real estate investing promoter and author of the bestselling book *Nothing Down*, Robert Allen, inveigled that same major newspaper in his own challenge stunt: taking a man at random out of the unemployment line and getting a home purchased in his name, with no credit used, and no money down, in a matter of days.

Even the simple proclamation made as if responding to a challenge like Harry Chandler's can lead to publicity. Once again, it was the *Los Angeles Times* that covered a Gary Halbert-engineered premiere event, where Tova Borgnine "swore under oath" that her new perfume contained no secret or illegal aphrodisiacs or sexual stimulants, despite its effects that would make one suspect such a thing!

The immediate publicity obtained by such activities is obviously valuable, but the person to person telling and re-telling of any one such story and an accumulated collection of such stories is a most powerful force. Also, in this day and age, publicity births more and more publicity in ways that John Brinkley had no access to, thanks to our 24/7 news media and online media, and its insatiable appetite for interesting stories. It's now common for a local story from Small-town, Kansas to migrate to national news. Given that such an environment exists, doesn't it seem that you should be actively striving to take advantage?

**HIGH VALUE QUESTION:** *what stories* ABOUT YOU *have you created, that are told and re-told by your customers and others, passed from one person to another?*

You may not be as brave as Dr. Brinkley in his sojourn to California, although there is something to be said (and admired) about the man or woman who "lays it all on the line" and risks success or failure in such a public fashion as with the Brinkley/Chandler *Los Angeles Times* challenge. There is every reason to believe that Harry Chandler would have demonized John R. Brinkley in print if the doctor's claims of sexual supremacy via goat gland transplantation had turned out to be an empty promise. Would you be willing to take such a risk? Would you dare manufacture such a risk?

Fortunately, creating a publicity friendly event in most local markets, especially in small, local markets does not require Brinkley-like boldness. One of my own consulting clients in the health care industry staged its own localized version of a popular television show and called it *The Lakebridge Idol*. What made it unique was that the amateur singing competition (open to all local residents) was held at an area nursing home, not a venue one would automatically think of for such high-jinx and fun. What ensued however was anything but foolish: fantastic public support, front page newspaper and television news coverage, and best of all from the client's perspective, the kind of publicity that translated into new residents coming to live in the facility. It isn't necessarily easy to get publicity for my clients like this, in the nursing home and assisted living industry—generally speaking, the owners and the media think of these as boring businesses. Yet, plenty of organic opportunities occur, like a resident celebrating her 100th birthday, winning some contest, hitting the lottery, being visited by a celebrity. The success of the *Lakebridge Idol* competition demonstrates no one need wait for the organic reason for media attention to occur.

Even at the peak of his success and prominence, Dr. Brinkley never stopped looking for and capitalizing on reasons for the public and the media to sit up and take notice of him, thus his trip to California and his association with Harry Chandler. Long before the rise of public relations as a profession and publicists routinely put on retainer, John Brinkley reportedly kept on his payroll no less than four men in different parts of the country (including the major cities of New York and Chicago) whose task was to keep him in front of reporters, editors, others in the media, and their readers.

Brinkley did his part here too, becoming a world traveler visiting far away nations, meeting with government leaders and talking up the benefits of his unique surgical procedures. The results included newspaper articles on a ruling monarch's upcoming visit from far away to little, old Milford, Kansas in order to receive his new goat glands.

While spending time in Los Angeles at Harry Chandler's request, John Brinkley was not content with meeting the challenge, and performing some profitable surgeries for the Hollywood crowd. He was impressed with the impact a story in the *Los Angeles Times* had, and even more impressed with the power Harry Chandler had, so he studied Chandler's operation.

In addition to owning a newspaper, Harry Chandler also owned a radio station. This is how Brinkley came upon the one medium that was to take him and his message into marketing superstardom.

Radio and Brinkley were made for each other. As already pointed out, the doctor's homespun common sense approach left a lasting impression on sex starved males and their equally frustrated wives. And best of all, Dr. Brinkley got to be both the writer and editor of his messages over the airwaves. There was no risk of being called a quack or a fake in print, and there was no chance of anyone disputing his claims or promises in an editorial. In addition, there was no one that was going to come on his radio station and challenge what he had to say to the masses. With this medium, he could exert total control.

Today, we have at hand many options offering this same kind of total control. You can buy your own radio program without owning a station, and there is Internet radio, still in its infancy, but showing promise. There are open channels of public communication and promotion where you have total control over your message with no editorial interference—such as YouTube, Facebook and blogs. There is the tried and true customer newsletter or proprietary magazine.

**The questions raised are**—what are you doing, to attract media and public attention, and to inspire people too talk about you and your exploits?

# 25

# Larger Than Life— And Then Some

*By Dan S. Kennedy*

I
n my books about The New Economy I advance the idea that, given the ever expanding array of choices consumers have in every category, and the recession training to be more judicious about choosing how to spend their money, **we've arrived at zero tolerance for anything ordinary. In concert, little tolerance for *anyone* ordinary.**

The greats have always understood that the public is best fascinated by somebody far from ordinary; larger than life. Truer today than ever, but a historical, evergreen, universal truth.

Ad man David Ogilvy arrived at client meetings elegantly dressed— and wearing a cape! As soon as he secured Rolls Royce as a client for his agency, he rushed to buy classic Rolls to be chauffeured in and park illegally, outside his New York office, even though, at the time, he could ill afford it. And he got custom plates OMB 2, OM for the agency, Ogilvy & Mather; the "2" suggesting the car might be the *second* Rolls in the fleet. Chip mentioned Dave Thomas. Dave became really interesting to the public and the media when his story line, orphan, school dropout, became known. Absent that, he was just another successful entrepreneur. An *ordinary*, successful entrepreneur. Even the creators of Superman were astute enough not to make him an ordinary superhero. Somehow they knew that just his super-powers and flamboyant costume would not be enough to sustain the public's interest. They created an origin story that made him an alien from a distant planet, gave him the emotional angst of a stranger in a strange land with curiosity and nostalgic longing for what he had lost, and a dangerous vulnerability to the space mineral Kryptonite. In short order, they had to switch from having Superman battle ordinary crooks to super-villains (a strategy borrowed outright by Ian Fleming for his James Bond novels).

Incidentally, there is a terrific novel, set in the 1930's; dealing with Superman's coming of age in a new way, which I urge you to read: *It's Superman* by Tom De Haven. I happen to a serious superhero buff, interested in the mythology and philosophy, but you need only casual awareness of the genre to enjoy this novel, and I think you might learn something from it. For more practical instruction, there is an audio program I recorded about all this, called *Personality in Copy/Creating Customers for Life*. (Available at DanKennedy.com)

**Looking backward, it's pretty obvious that Dr. John Brinkley deliberately fashioned himself as a larger than life figure, even as a super-hero.** He claimed a super power: the ability to perform a radical, miracle surgery that restored youthful/sexual vitality and erased many diseases of aging. He presented himself on a grand scale, with hospitals bearing his name (not an office), publicity stunts akin to racing a speeding bullet or stopping a speeding locomotive, he made himself the subject and star of books and movies, and at the earliest moment cash flow allowed, he surrounded himself with very visible trappings of wealth and prominence. Brinkley lived the first part of Shakespeare's line: "All the world's a stage…"

He even created his own cast of supporting characters. Superman had Jimmy Olsen, Lois Lane and others. He had the farmer, farmer's wife and Billy Jr., Happy Harry, his own deeply religious and therefore virtuous and trustworthy wife, and others. Finally, he had the drama of contest with villains; those in the medical establishment who would deny the public access to Brinkley's miracles if they could, out of envy, jealousy and ignorance.

These strategies are evident in many marketing scenarios around you today, if you know to look for them—but few use all of them as brilliantly as did Dr. Brinkley. But to name a couple modern examples…

Long ago sitcom actress playing a dumb blonde, Suzanne Somers, has made herself over, and has made a cottage industry around herself, as a champion of "alternative" health therapies including radical treatments for cancer, casting the harshly critical medical establishment as a villain bent on keeping the truth from the public, to protect its selfish interests; its turf; its profits. Her book, *KNOCKOUT: Interviews with Doctors Who Are Curing Cancer and How to Prevent It*, is representative of this story line, and she has been welcomed just about everywhere promoting it—from Larry King Live to Fox Business News to you name-it. In many ways, she is a version of Dr. John Brinkley, but entirely absent credentials. (Note use of the word 'cure'.)

When my client, the Guthy-Renker Corporation, plucked Tony Robbins out of relative obscurity, after discovering him and recognizing his charismatic ability when using him as a testimonial in their first infomercial for *Think And Grow Rich*, they introduced him to the public in his own infomercial, as a larger than life figure—with his own castle, helicopter, the requisite rags to riches story (apartment so small he washed his dishes in the bathtub). They surrounded him with a cast of celebrities giving testimony. Tony also had his own version of the goat glands transplant surgery: his ability to quickly strengthen anyone's mental toughness and mind control to point that they could walk barefoot across burning coals with no discomfort or burns.

There is a blueprint here, behind every one of these stories and behind John Brinkley's. It's laid out in full in the preceding Chapter and this one.

# PRINCIPLE #15

## BEING OF YOUR TIME, IN YOUR
# PLACE

# 26

# The Power of Time and Place

*By Chip Kessler*

**D**r. John R. Brinkley was born into poverty in the western hills of North Carolina, so poor, in fact, that it was a major motivating factor in first getting him out of his hometown of Beta, and then into some "enterprises" that would make a lot of money. He was, by family background, upbringing, and ready access to opportunity, unlikely to rise to fame and fortune—just as so many who do, are. This is an intriguing phenomenon, that so many of the richest and most celebrated entrepreneurs and business leaders, as well as entertainment celebrities, would have been judged Least Likely to Succeed by logic. There are the school dropouts, a long list that includes Dave Thomas, but also Bill Gates. Dr. Brinkley too, if you count his early exit from a questionable medical school. There are the very ordinary people who become extraordinary—think Sam Walton, as example. People who are minor players in cluttered, competitive fields, who claw their way out of the bottom tiers to rise to the very top. Oprah. What accounts for such individuals' not just making great sums of money, but also becoming legendary?

Certainly one factor is an extraordinary level of motivation and determination, often born of extreme disgust with the poverty they experience when young, and the vow to escape it and never return. Sometimes there is desire for grand success as revenge against critics, skeptics and doubters. Occasionally, such people are inspired by selfless mission. But more often by lust for conquest.

**Perhaps a more interesting and instructive, and less commonly talked and written about factor is these individuals' ability to uniquely capitalize on their time and place.**

Ponder this thought for a moment—how many legendary figures have risen, and how many fortunes have been made, by creating or co-opting, bringing forward and popularizing something initially met with enormous resistance or skepticism, just slightly ahead of its time. The telephone, television, the automobile, air travel. The Internet as a commercial media. The self-serve grocery store. The once entirely foreign concept of franchising pioneered by Colonel Sanders. Multi-level/network marketing. Dry cleaning. Sam Walton's small-markets-no-one-else-wanted strategy. X-ray machines. Transplant surgery. Vitamins. Television, daytime talk shows invading soap opera territory. Reality TV. Online, the swap meet moved to E-Bay, the department store to Amazon. Behind most such inventions or popularization, a personality made by each invention or popularization, a fortune, usually followed by many fortunes, even entirely new industries.

Incidentally, John Brinkley did not invent goat gland transplantation surgery. It existed before he became its champion and promoter, and popularized it, and made himself famous and rich in the process. Many inventions languished in relative oblivion before a John Brinkley found them and successfully promoted them.

In every such case, there have been time and place factors favoring the successful promoter.

Brinkley first arrived on the scene with full force in the period following World War I and several years before the Great Depression. It was a coming of age in America, known as "The Roaring Twenties." The United States was beginning to really feel its oats. Automobiles were replacing horse-drawn carriages on American streets, and liberating people to travel greater distances with some measure of efficiency. There was nightlife; there were party girls known as "flappers" and people danced the Charleston. In general, there was a "live it up" type of lifestyle that for its day would go unrivaled for its openness and sexual nature until the free love generation of the 1960's. There was a national optimism and embracing of the new, to point of mass gullibility. There was conspicuous consumption, comparable to that of our 1990's.

In this environment arose Dr. John R. Brinkley ready to fix what ailed a man! Indeed, in this period of anything goes, live-it-up, drink-it-down revelry why should a man have to forgo one of life's greatest pleasures ... when the Brinkley Institute of Health in the heartland of America was there to provide it?

Arguably, a handful of years earlier or a handful of years later, John Brinkley would have found it much more difficult to create and launch himself as he did. It is likely true that the fact that he already had traction and momentum permitted him to proceed through the Depression and still prosper. Clearly, his quick recognition of the power of media in its infancy, and his aggressive exploitation of it, made major contribution to his success. Brinkley's beginnings in a small town, heartland of America location also worked to his advantage, connecting him in the public's mind with strong, traditional values and trustworthiness. Had he been a fancy-pants doctor from the big city, things might have turned out differently.

It can be said that John Brinkley was a man of and for his time and his place.

**This begs the question**: are you positioning and presenting yourself as a person of your time and place?

Some themes are deeply ingrained in our culture, and seem to never change. But other cultural attitudes, mores and interests change considerably. As we were writing this book, retired General Colin Powell came forward to advocate the repeal of the don't-ask, don't-tell policy governing gays and lesbians serving in the military, closeted vs. openly; a policy he had championed seventeen years ago. His explanation for his reversal: much in the public attitude has changed in those seventeen years. Yes, it has. As have changes in attitudes about aging, retirement, and later years of life—which I deal with in the industry I consult in and invest in. As, probably, have attitudes about your field of endeavor. It's important not to get "locked in" to a view of the consumer you market to, but to recognize that his mind-set is fluid not fixed, his interests changing, his needs and desires evolving.

How much do you follow current trends and the public's reaction to them? No matter the era or decade, there is always something that's catching the public's fancy. Sometimes, it is something fleeting, other times, something new that has real staying power. This is true about *what* people are willing or eager to buy as well as *how* they are willing or eager to buy.

As the nation ramped up in the 1920's, Brinkley did likewise. He aggressively used direct mail. He was among the first to determine that patients would travel great distances to seek the services of a celebrated specialist. One of the first of what Dan Kennedy calls "no boundaries marketers". Among the first to realize that people would "buy" a doctor at a distance, thanks to that doctor talking to them via the radio airwaves rather than in person. He was on the forefront of change in what people would buy, who they would buy it from, and how they would buy. Are you?

# Where Is Your Place?
# When Is Your Time?

*By Dan S. Kennedy*

**M**y place is in print. I trained myself to perform well and function successfully in other places, notably on stage, as a speaker, somewhat of an entertainer, and as a pitchman... in one on one, face to face selling situations... in probative consulting sessions—although most effectively with solo entrepreneurs, least effectively with corporate bureaucrats and committees. But my true, best, most productive place is in print and print media. I am not, for example, personally effective in video or on TV. I struggle there. I'm not very effective in teleseminars. I don't like the phone, and my energy quickly wanes when using it. I am at my best with the written word, in print. This I have come to accept, understand and embrace. *To embrace my place.*

John Brinkley began as a medicine show pitchman, because that was the only example he'd seen that appeared to offer escape from poverty and small town drudgery. But he came to the realization that, by far and away, his place was radio. As it is today for, say, Rush Limbaugh. As TV with a live audience has been for Oprah. As pitching to home viewers and kibitzing with callers has been for Joan Rivers, on QVC. The classic, late-night TV talk show, the Carson-like Tonight Show (with some Steve Allen thrown in) has proved a fabulous place for Letterman, but basically doing the same Dave Letterman, he failed miserably with a mid-morning, daytime talk show. Once, California was the place for personal development, metaphysical and spiritual gurus to flourish, and cult-ish, organically grown, sell-it-by-zealot programs like EST thrived. Today, at the moment, Asia seems a more welcoming place for the current version of the success and self-improvement movement. At one point in time, the places retirees migrated to en masse were Florida and, to lesser degree, Arizona. While that migration remains significant, college towns offering lively cultural environments and stay-young encouragement, urban downtowns offering everything within walking distance and zero maintenance, high rise living, and places like North Carolina offering gentle climates are attracting, and actively marketing to, baby boomer retirees and semi-retirees.

These are all examples of the impact of place on success.

Brinkley would almost certainly never have reached his extraordinary heights of wealth and celebrity without his self-developed use of the media, his placement of self in media, and, in particular, his placement of self in radio. He would probably have spent his entire life as a small-time, itinerant grifter, and quite possibly spent some of it behind bars in different towns' jails.

Had I not gravitated to print, recognized it as my place, and devoted my primary attention to developing my writing ability and my use of print media, I imagine I would need to be endlessly on the road, selling something to some groups of some bodies, absent any stability or security, let alone celebrity.

I think it is very important to determine where your most productive place is, and then to make it the chief object of your study and personal and professional development, and to leverage your committed marriage to it, to the greatest extent possible.

## *Somewhere, There's The Perfect Place For Everybody. It Often Isn't The Obvious Place Or First Place Entered.*

A particular *media* constitutes place. **Subject matter** is another place. In my case, for example, I began talking and writing about self-improvement and personal development, but found it a very cluttered place in which differentiation was difficult, and for the stage, a more charismatic personality than mine was desirable. I am not now and certainly was not then a mesmerist. Further, that subject matter was not a good path to high fee, one on one consultative relationships, let alone to copywriting project work, which ultimately provided the greatest income opportunity for me. I found my best subject-matter place in marketing, and more narrowly, direct marketing.

Suzanne Somers, mentioned in an earlier Chapter, found it in radical, alternative health. Jon Stewart, once an ordinary stand-up comedian, found it in political satire. If you think this does not apply to you because you are an insurance agent or investment advisor or operate a restaurant or own a manufacturing company, you're wrong. You are thinking un-creatively. Everybody has, or can and should have, subject matter about which they pontificate and advocate, in order to be endlessly interesting to a market.

Which brings me to another place: **market.** Again using myself as example, my best market place is with the entrepreneurial-minded, politically conservative or libertarian small business owner or sales professional. *Not* with corporate types. *Not* with the MBA crowd. *Not* with academics. And *not* with committed liberals, militant feminists or the extremely metaphysical. To quote Eastwood from a movie: a man's got to know his limitations.

**HIGH VALUE QUESTION:** *where is* YOUR *most productive Place?*

Everybody has some constituency they resonate with and some constituency they repel, and everybody can strengthen, embellish, exaggerate and emphasize whatever about them resonates and repels, for magnetic effect. John Brinkley certainly did it: his ideal patient was a middle-aged or older married man, a working man, or a more affluent self-made farm or business owner who spoke plainly and appreciated plain-speaking, and tended to distrust scholarly academics and big city elites, and to some extent, the establishment. Brinkley knew his place and did everything to flourish there, without worry over how much he was criticized and reviled in places that were not his.

**Time is another matter altogether, yet inter-related with place**. I have often said that the only difference between salad and garbage is timing, but that it's impossible to actually control timing—such as the moment a particular person develops sufficient need and emotional readiness to buy a particular product. In a narrow sense, that requires being frequently present with generally qualified prospects, or to identify a timing 'sweet spot' you can target market to, most typically with direct-mail. For example, I learned that, in the hearing aid business, an ideal prospect is a widower or widow between 50 and 65 years old, reached six months after the spouse's death. In the first months, he or she mourns; in the four to five month neighborhood, he or she re-socializes, and realizes that their "human hearing aid" has been lost. For the weight loss center, cosmetic surgeon and cosmetic dentist: a divorced woman age 40 to 60, about four months after the divorce, who got the house. Were Dr. Brinkley alive and selling his goat glands transplants, I imagine he might find a middle-aged man post-divorce or older, affluent man just married to a trophy wife half his age to be ideal prospects.

But in a bigger, broader sense, the public consciousness changes with time. America is still a right-of-center, slightly conservative nation, and probably always will be, at least fiscally, if more moderate on social issues, because, as Ronald Reagan said, everybody's a liberal when young; they get more conservative as they acquire things to conserve. There will always be a next generation arriving at that place in time. At times, we briefly move far to the left, at other times far to the right, for we are a reactionary people. But we always return to the near middle.

In presidential politics, it's hard to succeed if not pandering to the left or right extreme during party primaries, but equally hard to succeed if you can't or won't move back to the middle in the general election, and in the few cases a true ideologue manages election, he experiences fast and dramatic failure if trying to govern from far left or right. Of course, socio-economic-political attitudes and values vary by demographics, by geographic locale, by occupation, by upbringing, gender, race and numerous other factors. It should be noted that John Brinkley grew more and more outspoken as a far-right conservative in philosophy, presumably as he learned more and more about the attitudes of his ideal prospect, "the self-made man".

There are times when people are irrationally exuberant, and then tend to spend very freely and indiscriminately, accumulate debt without concern, invest aggressively and in the new and unproven, and tend to be "out and about" with abandon. Brinkley's Roaring Twenties. Our own 2000 to 2006 or so. There are other times when people are anxious and worried, or angry and anti-establishment, irrationally pessimistic, and tend toward the trend originally termed "cocooning" by analyst Faith Popcorn. It's important to match your positioning and your marketing messages to current and evolving time conditions.

There was a time when aging gracefully and appropriately was expected and honored, and contrary behavior looked upon critically. We now live in a time when denying and defying age, and fighting it every step of the way; when dressing, dating, marrying, and acting in very age inappropriate ways is not only accepted but celebrated. It's cool, for example, to be a "cougar". It wasn't that long ago that it was pathetic. To use this as example, and to narrow to advertising, if I'm choosing photos for a cosmetic surgeon, I'll now show an older woman with a younger man; a half-decade ago, I would show her with a healthy, good-looking man of her same age. You might think that John Brinkley's promise of youthful vitality at any age was in contradiction to his time, but that would reveal lack of depth of understanding of the American attitudes of that time. The most significant attitudinal dynamic of that window in time was not tradition; it was embrace of self-determination vs. pre-ordained destiny. And it was a time of fast and dramatic change and innovation, including technological (think: auto) and medical innovation, so acceptance of Brinkley's Big Idea fit.

In short, you can't control time or timing, but you can get in sync with your time. You can, in essence, be a person of your time, a voice of your time. This requires you to understand what the people you market to are just getting ready to accept, to be eager to hear, and to be there with that message and those ideas as their readiness "boils".

This sensitivity and thoughtfulness about place and time is a relatively sophisticated aspect of marketing, beyond what most businesspeople engage themselves in. In studying Brinkley, I'm convinced he was not at all an accidental phenom of his place and time, but that he was conscious and deliberate. Anyone can be. Few are.

---

Special Note: I would be remiss in writing about Place, and Place as a marketing strategy, without mentioning a client and friend, and fellow author, one of the world's reigning authorities on this subject, Stephen Roulac, author of PLACE AND PROPERTY STRATEGY. Stephen is the CEO of an investment group, a "place strategies advisor" to leading companies, has hosted his own show on NPR, and been cited in virtually every significant financial publication, including Forbes and Kiplinger's. While I had focused on "place" in broader terms than geographic location and as marketing strategy before encountering Stephen, my evolved, current thinking on the subject has been profoundly influenced by his work. You can access his thinking at www.roulac.com

# PRINCIPLE #16

## MAKING WHATEVER YOU'VE GOT,

# WORK

# 28

# Making Lemonade from Lemons

*By Chip Kessler*

Perhaps no one is better at making "lemonade from lemons" than politicians and their spin-misters. Leave it to one of our elected officials to literally step in dog poop and he will claim it was a good thing "because by doing this Senator so-and-so was able to get this blight on the public's eyes and stench to the public's nose off the street." In February of 2010, the President's Secretary of Education actually did say that Hurricane Katrina was the best thing to ever happen to the New Orleans public school system, by making re-development and reform possible. Perhaps the instinct to spin to such extent ought to be curbed!

Entrepreneurs, however, are less famous for spinning, and more certain to *actually convert* lemons to lemonade, adversity to opportunity. John Brinkley took whatever he had to work with at any given moment and made the best of it, and when handed a significantly disadvantageous situation, found a way to exploit it as a marketing or promotional opportunity.

**This is the way we entrepreneurs must think.**

As example, consider this difference between an entrepreneurial response vs. a corporate response to a crisis. In 1998, Bill Glazer, now President of Glazer-Kennedy Insider's Circle™, the largest association of marketing-oriented entrepreneurs in the world, was still operating his original business, independent menswear stores. His main store was flooded by a malfunctioning sprinkler system, with some goods ruined, others just wet but when dried out, intact and perfectly wearable. Upon discovering his store knee-deep in water, Bill sprang into action. He created a newspaper advertisement about the incident, and used it as excuse for a special sales event. You can see that ad and read a bit more about it in Dan Kennedy's introduction to Bill's book, *Outrageous Advertising*. That's an entrepreneur. In 2010, Toyota was confronted with a crisis of customer confidence, spurred by a multi-million car recall necessitated by defects in gas pedal, braking and electronic systems, causing some cars to accelerate uncontrollably and others to refuse to stop. As we were writing this book, the company had gone from denial and downplaying of the problem to coping with it, but there was no sign of them jumping on it as excuse for a promotion! That's a corporate bureaucracy.

If he was anything, John Brinkley was an entrepreneur.

John Brinkley did visit some of the major cities of the United States, and performed his goat gland transplant surgery in these venues, however the majority of his medical work took place in three locations, where he established his own hospitals: Milford, Kansas; Del Rio, Texas; and Little Rock, Arkansas. The first was somewhat by happenstance, but the second and third were choices forced upon him by trouble in the present spot, and economic pressures. None of these destinations was going to be mistaken for New York City, Chicago or Los Angeles. Population-wise, the three towns wouldn't compare with Kansas City, Houston or Dallas either. On the surface, it would seem that a doctor promoting a modern, breakthrough surgical procedure would be expected to reside in a major metropolis, not a backwoods small town. And surely getting people to travel to these off-the-main-path towns would put up a barrier to success.

But John Brinkley adapted the manner in which he presented himself to the locations he placed his clinics in. The Brinkley marketing machine paid ample homage to the fact that the doctor's somewhat remote setting facilitated the dedicated man at work, far removed from the hustle and bustle of the big city, where distractions were aplenty and his attention to his on-going research and the important surgery he was performing wouldn't receive its just due. He utilized his isolated locations to further his mystique, not harm it.

*Photograph of Dr. Brinkley's impressive hospital
in Little Rock, Arkansas.*

## BRINKLEY BUILT WITH WHATEVER BRICKS HE HAD. DO YOU?

Most unsuccessful, frustrated businesspeople can recite circumstantial reasons for their failure, a list that often includes location. *If only I was in a bigger market... in Beverly Hills or Manhattan... could afford to have my store in the big mall...* and so on. If not this excuse, another. My co-author says if you're determined to excuse failure, one excuse is just as useful as any other.

Consider, again, location as object lesson. Do your marketing materials paint a picture of why you are located where you are, and the reasons it just happens to be the very best place for you to do what you do? Dan Kennedy has painted a very clear picture of why his home base is in a small town near Cleveland, Ohio. Dan's "picture" includes the facts that it is his home region where he grew up, and that his love of harness racing (and participation as a harness racing driver at a local track which holds fond memories to him) are the major reasons he is where he is, having moved back there, in fact, from the much sunnier, warmer, bigger city of Phoenix. Dan also glamorizes small town life, and small town values, when he writes or speaks about his location.

It is *not* a "natural". Since almost all of Dan's clients and coaching groups must travel to him, and some companies even hold their conferences in Dan's home city so Dan will agree to appear as a speaker, there are obviously any number of places Dan could reside that would be more appealing to visit or to hold a meeting at. The list of places that would be less off-putting, easier to get to, more centrally located, or in much better climates is quite long. But Dan is there and has made a personal, lifestyle choice to be there, so he makes the best of it. He uses it as a teaching example, for principles of autonomy, independence, and the power of category-of-one positioning. He draws stories and humor from it. To visiting groups and seminar attendees, he offers the added experience of visiting the racetrack, taking a backstage tour, meeting and being photographed with racehorses, and an evening at the races in the clubhouse. How many of us would put Cleveland on our list of top ten places to visit before we die if Dan were not there? Few. But how many of us would jump at the chance to go there "to meet with the wizard" if invited—even if in the dead of winter fraught with sub-zero temperatures and six feet of snow? Many.

John R. Brinkley decided early in his "surgical career" to turn Milford, Kansas into his personal Mecca for the men that craved his service, and make it known far and wide as the home of the most amazing medical treatments and miracles of the time. He deliberately modeled his Milford hospital after the finest such establishments that Great Brittan had to offer. Brinkley, however, didn't stop there. As Pope Brock reports in *Charlatan*, the erstwhile doctor also added a coat of arms (with a knight, shield, flowers and golden colored vines) and got a newspaper photo that featured the one and only J. R. Brinkley strolling the grounds with his pet, an English water spaniel. He mailed out tens of thousands of brochures detailing how the Brinkley medical campus was the Kansas equivalent of jolly old England itself, with a superior combination of modern medical breakthroughs set against the peace and tranquility of gracious countryside living. As a big fish in a small town, Brinkley's hospital dominated its downtown; the comings and goings of his patients filled the train station; his every new pronouncement made news. Because he so controlled the town, he was able to give his patients a unique and memorable experience, certain to be talked about back home. By objective standards, his Milford base, and his subsequent two locations, were not "naturally" advantageous, but he made them so.

As Brinkley's fame spread and his audacity in his marketing grew, he, of course, fell under greater and more ardent attack from skeptics, critics and regulatory agents. The details of this, ultimately contributing to 'the fall of John Brinkley' part of the story are told in good detail in Pope Brock's book, so we've chosen not to cover that same ground here. What is instructive, though, is that every time a seemingly negative incident or new threat came John Brinkley's way, he responded to it just as he did to opening his clinic's doors in little Milford, Kansas. He used whatever was thrown at him as opportunity to grow his legend, attract publicity, better bond with or fascinate his audience, and promote his services. To John Brinkley, everything was raw material for the manufacture of more prominence, promotion and patient flow.

# PRINCIPLE #17

BEING ADMIRED AS A
## FIGHTER

# 29

# What *Will* You Do— To Succeed?

## *By Chip Kessler*

For over 20 years, I was a radio sportscaster. During this period, I got to rub shoulders with a lot of college football and basketball coaches, and even spent some time covering Major League Baseball's Atlanta Braves. Coaches would always tell me that they would much rather have an athlete of limited talent, who works hard and will do anything and everything he can to be a good ballplayer, than one with such exceptional talent the athlete felt that alone should carry the day. It might seem odd to hear a coach insist he'd rather have a less talented player than might be available, yet I heard the same sentiment expressed by many, and acted on by many as they recruited and jettisoned different players.

The making all that you can out of whatever you have to work with, no waiting, no excuses, which I wrote about in the preceding Chapter is a matter of attitude, not aptitude.

**There is much to be said for "fire in the belly."**

So it was with Dr. John R. Brinkley. He had absolutely zilch given to him and had to fight for everything he got. He came from poverty. He had negligible formal education. Because of the controversial nature of his most promoted surgical procedure as well as most of his philosophy and recommendations about health, Brinkley traveled "under a black cloud", criticized, scorned and reviled by the medical establishment, and bedeviled by skeptics within the media he needed to exploit, who were determined to expose him as a fraud. He never found Easy Street. Nonetheless, John Brinkley was able to scheme, invent, and create marketing and promotion strategies that were, for an extended term, virtually unstoppable, and to quite literally pull himself up from oblivion and poverty to fame and fortune. He was reportedly the wealthiest doctor of his time, certainly at peak a multi, multi-millionaire.

Many factors made this possible. A key one: John Brinkley's own mind-set. If we dissect his thinking, as we have throughout this book, as one might dissect a body in the laboratory, we find it complex, not simple. As discussed in the last Chapter, Brinkley disciplined himself to think of circumstances as opportunities, not adversities. He became so convinced of his own powers of persuasion, communication and survivability; he was bold not timid, and daring not cautious. Animals can be divided into two types: fight or flee. Brinkley was a fighter, a warrior, combative and aggressive. Almost any of these, if possessed in insufficient volume or in excess, can be hazardous if not harmful. Those who succeed at the levels John Brinkley did, and sustain success at a level John Brinkley could not, have just the right mix. Dangerous amounts, managed.

The difficult task comes when we each try to assess and evaluate our own mind-set, to identify and strengthen weaknesses, to get to the right mix. Those I got to know in the world of sports, and those I've gotten to know in the business world since, have made me realize it is a volatile mix. Certainly, one of the best measures of it is in a person's response to different challenges to his plans and progress, goals and objectives.

What do *you* do when…

➤ Facing some stiff competition from other businesses or marketers that have already staked out a claim in the field or marketplace you are entering?

➤ Having to battle well-meaning family or friends who tell you that you are bucking insurmountable odds and will fail, at least implying if not stating that you are just not up to the challenge?

➤ Dealing with money/financing problems?

➤ Encountering disappointing and insufficient response from customers or prospects to your products, services or propositions?

➤ Confronting criticism and critics, authorities who tell you that you "can't" proceed as intended, or gossip and rumor-mongers polluting your marketplace?

➤ Needing to overcome a setback or a series of setbacks?

With all these things, it's not really a question of "if", only a question of "when". The entire list and more and worse will happen to every entrepreneur attempting to accomplish much of anything. It's axiomatic that the push for exceptional innovation, achievement or prominence attracts opposition. To expect anything else is naive. The pay-off, though, is that the world stops and pays attention to the person who can withstand and triumph over attack or adversity. The person who runs, with tail between legs, usually sacrifices self-respect, the respect of others, and power, permanently. The person who battles back and fights may be badly bruised from time to time, but often also earns great respect and commands great power.

Success lore is full of these stories. How Tom Monaghan almost lost control of Dominos thanks to monstrous financial and management misjudgments, but stayed, and fought, and won. Donald Trump wrote about his own fall and rise, in "*The Art of the Comeback*.' Martha Stewart, humiliated, sent to prison. Her brand badly damaged. But back on top, more successful and popular than ever. Post-*prison*. In reviewing the entire life of John Brinkley, it is clear that he lived by the philosophy that the only real failure was surrender. You have to ask yourself, what core philosophy do you live by?

## *Okay, World—I'll Accept Your Wager and Raise The Stakes*

One of the most interesting behaviors of super-entrepreneurs confronted and challenged by some set of adverse circumstances is that they often choose to "up the ante".

In 1930, in conflict with Kansas state government over his medical practice, John R. Brinkley threw his wide brimmed hat into the ring for Governor of the state of Kansas running as an independent, write-in candidate. Instead of just fighting the fight he was already in, he picked a new, bigger fight!

Marketing-wise Brinkley's gubernatorial campaign was every bit up to the standards he'd previously established, which enabled him to become the nation's unquestioned leader in goat-gland transplant surgery. In running for the state's highest office, Brinkley was the first political candidate in the United States to do such things as:

✓ Travel to destinations in an airplane—and not just any airplane mind you, but an aircraft that was previously owned by Charles Lindbergh

✓ Broadcast his political philosophy and wisdom over his radio station KFKB—becoming the earliest politician to use this particular medium

Would someone else eventually have used radio and travel by airplane for the same purpose? The answer certainly is yes, however credit and praise must be duly given to the man that first thought of the idea. Someone else besides Thomas Edison would've surely invented electricity and someone else besides Alexander Graham Bell would've eventually invented the telephone. But we give them their due.

John Brinkley was the first in his field to modernize the way politicians traveled to drum up votes and the method politicians employed to communicate with the masses. The end results: Brinkley could travel to see more voters in a day than his rivals, and he could speak to even more voters via the radio.

Brinkley campaigned as an anti-establishment populist, and as an angry man, a surrogate for the frustration and rage felt by every-man. This should sound very, very familiar.

Did Brinkley win his race for Governor? No he did not. Brinkley wound up third, some 33,000 votes behind the Democratic and Republican candidates (who were in a tight race themselves separated by less than 200 votes at the end). Yet as Pope Brock recounts in the book *Charlatan* from a report in the *Des Moines Register*, the goat-gland country doctor from little Milford, Kansas came about as close as one could to winning the Governor's chair:

*"Were in not for the fact that one in six of his supporters failed to write his name correctly on the ballot, Dr. John R. Brinkley, the goat-gland specialist … would today be governor-elect of Kansas. Brinkley garnered more than 183,000 votes, without having his name on the ballot, and it is estimated that from 30,000 to 50,000 others intended to vote for him but spoiled their ballots by mistake."*

Sounds a bit like the hanging chads episode in Florida, doesn't it?

As the report states, many Brinkley enthusiasts did not correctly write out the candidate's name in the proper form and fashion (the Kansas Election Board had previously ruled that the candidate's name must be written exactly as J.R. Brinkley and nothing else). Instead tens of thousands of voters wrote "Doctor Brinkley" or "Doc Brinkley." Some other stalwarts may have written his name in as it was supposed to be, but then disqualified their ballots by listing J.R. Brinkley as their choice for jobs such as U.S. Senator, Kansas Supreme Court Justice or even U.S. Supreme Court Justice. Thus despite Brinkley's efforts to educate the Kansas voters on how to properly write in his name on the ballot, he lost his bid.

But Brinkley's venture into politics had other benefits. It temporarily quelled attempts to put his hospital out of business. And it was a publicity bonanza. Newspapers such as the *New York Times* and the aforementioned *Des Moines Register* as well as every newspaper in Kansas carried accounts of his political efforts, and all naturally played up Brinkley's status as the famous goat glands transplant surgeon, claiming to restore sexual vitality to men of all ages, even into their 80's. There is no telling how many patients found their way to Dr. Brinkley as a result, but it's a safe wager there were many.

You might not wish to pick a political fight or run for political office, but you might, instead, become the champion of a charity or cause, as Dave Thomas did for adoption and for education; as Paul Newman tied a burgeoning food empire to charitable activity. Donald Trump has not been above picking fights timed with need for publicity, including much publicized battles with Rosie O'Donnell, Mayor Bloomberg and *Forbes Magazine*. He also once threatened to run for President; with enough conviction it became a subject of media speculation, keeping him the news for weeks. In a small, local market, running for dog-catcher may be enough political ambition to bring notoriety, picking a public fight with an extremely unpopular politician risky but profitable, or championing the cause of a tiny charity or even one abandoned dog enough to make you a hero.

The point of all this is: what *will* you do to promote yourself and your business, to succeed at a level others don't? Will you "put yourself out there" in ways that other businesspeople fear, aren't capable of doing, or are unwilling to invest the extra effort in?

# 30

# Put Your Dukes Up

*By Dan S. Kennedy*

I'd like to share some personal experiences and insights that link to the preceding two Chapters. For the many readers who know me and follow me, this may give you new or different insight into the strategy behind what you see.

**I have been picking fights for promotion and profit my entire life**, although, miraculously, I've never actually taken or thrown a punch in a physical altercation.

Over years, for example, I collected a great deal of money from peers; professional speakers and authors who I reached because they and I were members of the National Speakers Association, the leading trade organization in that field. I "made my bones" there, and attracted the attention I needed, by picking fights with the Association itself. I criticized the traditional business models it stood for, preached and memorialized with its awards as antiquated, imbecilic, narrow, and hazardous to one's

**185**

mental health and personal wealth. I made fun of its alphabet-soup certifications and designations that no one outside the clan cared one whit about, and that required somebody to be so bad they were never invited back by the same group to qualify for them. I cautioned against the tired old dogs lecturing the new young pups, given that the old dogs were in competition with the young pups, jealous of them, and scared of them. I criticized the entire culture of the association. I made a lot of enemies, I got a reputation as a brash and arrogant prick (and, with some, as a breath of fresh truth), and I got known, watched, talked about and gossiped about. And I resonated with and attracted the business-oriented members who had already known most of what they were being fed was B.S., and couldn't be happier to have somebody arrive who dared say so. I will never forget one of the "big name" well respected old guard guys coming to me rather sheepishly and asking for consulting days if I would solemnly pledge to keep his working with me a secret!

That fight even included my being tossed out of the association, having to sue and win court-ordered reinstatement.

I have always picked a fight with pinhead academics and theorists writing or lecturing or consulting about business—even though they've never actually run one and wouldn't last a week off campus, taking fire on the business battlefield. Same with honchos at big, dumb corporations daring to lecture small business owners and entrepreneurs about how things ought to be done, even as their behemoths post massive losses. Sales trainers who sell only in their memories. If you'd like a quick look at this kind of fight-picking, check out Chapter 1 in *No B.S. Business Success In The New Economy*, Chapter 1 in *No B.S. Ruthless Management of People and Profits*, and Chapter 19 in *No B.S. Sales Success In The New Economy*.

To give you a hint, Chapter 19 is titled 'B.S. That Sales Managers Shovel Onto Salespeople.' My sarcastic attacks on these targets win me the hearts 'n minds, approval and applause, and trust of true entrepreneurs.

I have routinely picked fights with people espousing avoidance of work. I pick this fight for two reasons. One, I think this is damaging not just to the fools drinking this Kool-Aid®, but to society as a whole. Two, because my best customers and clients have strong work ethic and despise the something-for-nothing idea, so my attacks repel those who'll be lousy customers, and attract the best ones.

I pick fights with liberals and socialists and destroyers, those who attack capitalism and demonize the rich, and I have specifically picked fights with Michael Moore, the President, and Chris Matthews of MSNBC. You can see one of my jabs at Matthews on pages 218-221 of *No B.S. Business Success in the New Economy*. You can also read my weekly political rant at BusinessAndMedia. org. Unfortunately, my publishers' publicists have had their collective heads up their butt about converting my positions taken in these books into actual confrontations with the Moores and Mathews of the world, so publicity has been scarce. But in terms of resonating with my intended audience; my ideal customers, this is a worthy battle of words to wage.

The entrepreneur feels disrespected, demonized, misunderstood and put upon by government and media elites, and having me champion the cause and throw some punches in print, it pleases them greatly.

Dr. Brinkley quickly discovered the value of being "for" his patients, for the working man, for the self-made man, and on larger scale as time went on, "for" truth and freedom, and "against" the medical

**FROM THE BRINKLEY BLUEPRINT:**
*Being "for", and being "against".*

188 **Chapter Thirty** *Put Your Dukes Up*

establishment, over-bearing and intrusive government, interference with individuals' rights—including the right to get goat's glands' aid for erections lasting longer than four hours. His running for Governor was a natural, evolutionary extension of his position as champion of and fighter for "the people."

**It's a very good thing to ask yourself**: whether "your people" see you as their champion, fighting for them? Key word: fighting.

I have also fought my way through my fair share of crap and adversity, some self-induced, some delivered by others, in order to achieve what I've achieved, and not only do I make no secret of any of that, I am nakedly open about it, to a degree, boastful about it. My regular readers, students, followers, customers, clients are very much aware of my stuttering as a child, my 'Rich Dad, Poor Dad, Same Dad' experiences with poverty, my very serious boozing, my bankruptcies, my close association with an enormously talented empire-builder with sufficient flaws in his make-up he landed in prison, my divorce, the disrespect of my peers, and, well, need we include the *whole* list here? I share all my "doing whatever it takes" stories, and I have many. I believe I succeed at conveying a sense of myself as a warrior, a fighter, a conqueror. Maybe something of a "Rocky." I strive to convey that for others' benefit, because it is motivational, but also, of course, for my benefit because—make a note of this—people more willingly give money to somebody they *admire*.

John Brinkley understood this thoroughly. As you examine his literature, radio broadcasts, etc.—the samples in this book, and the greater quantity of samples in the complete home study course on Brinkley marketing, you'll see how he casts himself as champion and fighter for the people, and, in general, as a fighter to be admired.

*When campaigning for Governor,*
*John Brinkley even had his own stamps produced!*

# PRINCIPLE #18

## CREATING POWERFUL
# POSITIONING

# 31

# Maximum-Strength Positioning

*By Chip Kessler*

One of the phenomenon's we live by these days is those folks who are able to become as the term goes, "famous for being famous."

There's 'the heiress" who prances around the globe with this boyfriend or that one, and who even got her own television show that ran for a few years. Then there are 'the daughters" that have their own cable "reality" show who face the kinds of *problems* that most people who really have problems would love to have. The cable TV universe is a bottomless pit of need for programming, and there is no shortage of people eager to get and stretch their 15 minutes of fame willing to take their turns leaping into the pit. Some, like Snookie from The Jersey Shore—the number one show on MTV in 2009—parlay their fame-for-being-famous into income, from the show, from appearance fees from night-clubs and private events, even book deals (thus providing employment for ghost-

193

writers). Overall, though, the business of being famous for being famous gives most very fragile and short-lived opportunity.

John R. Brinkley wasn't famous for being famous. Rather he gained fame, fortune and notoriety to a certain extent for being infamous ... and it was something he didn't run away from. Brinkley was smart enough and a savvy enough student of human interest to realize that controversy sells. It's possible that John Brinkley got as much negative press as positive, and were he transplanted into the modern world with the internet, we can be certain there would be plenty of anti-Brinkley chatter all over social media and even at web sites designated to the express purpose of bashing him. If you are very visible at all, and an aggressive promoter of anything, you are very likely the subject of such online attacks—from disgruntled customers, jealous competitors and their surrogates, possibly others. When you examine the life of Dr. Brinkley, you can draw different conclusions about how he responded then, and how he would probably respond in today's environment. You could conclude that he might better have been more restrained in his enthusiasm for his own infamy and more careful about creating determined enemies. You might recognize how much of his success was fueled by public awareness and curiosity created for him, by those doggedly pursuing and attacking him. You might be inspired to more strategically create and leverage criticism, controversy and even enemies.

Given the nature of his #1 product, controversy was inevitable. After all, Dr. Brinkley wasn't the physician you went to if you had a broken leg or a sore throat. He welded goat glands—or if you were affluent enough—human glands to men's private parts, to re-ignite virility. Even in today's environment, where organ transplants are accepted, common medical procedures, and save many lives every year; and the enhancement of the body's appearance with surgically added or re-shaped parts is as widely marketed and accepted as lipstick purchased at Walgreen's, Dr. Brinkley's chosen procedure would bring intense scrutiny and the wrath of the regulatory community to his doorstep. But in the early 1900's, with no established acceptance for transplant or cosmetic surgery, there was no possibility of promoting what he did as he did without drawing enemy fire.

In John Brinkley's case, the American Medical Association, then growing in power, found him to be the ideal target. Actually the AMA waged a number of battles against Brinkley through the years, starting with challenging his credentials to even perform surgery in the first place. The end result was that the Dr. Brinkley was destined to spend ample time and money having to defend himself in court. Brinkley did his level best to make that a profitable investment rather than the road to ruin, and for quite some time, was successful at doing so.

His drama did not just include a nameless, faceless bureaucracy, though. It featured a determined individual for whom battle with Brinkley became intensely personal, and a life's mission. Brinkley was the target, a truly hated target, of one of America's first self-proclaimed protectors of the public's interest and consumer advocates, Dr. Morris Fishbein. You might think of him as the Ralph Nader of the 1920's. Fishbein used his pulpit, as first associate editor and then editor of the *Journal of the American Medical Association,* to wage a one-man campaign against Brinkley. He relentlessly pursued Brinkley for more than a decade, publishing expose after expose in his own media, giving countless newspaper interviews, speeches, even writing anti-Brinkley pamphlets and books for broad distribution, as well as haranguing state governments and regulatory bodies to put Brinkley out of business. Fishbein made himself famous as a consumer advocate and prosecutor of medical frauds, by making Dr. Brinkley infamous. Without the Corvair and General Motors, Nader's first bestselling book *Unsafe at Any Speed* would never have been possible. As GM made Nader, Brinkley made Fishbein.

John Brinkley was never cowed by Fishbein's attacks. Instead Brinkley would acknowledge and use Fishbein's print attacks in the AMA Journal and elsewhere, to position himself as type of doctor who was so committed to helping the common man that he was willing to courageously battle the short-sighted, dim-witted, thumb-sucking, didn't-know-a-cure-if-it- bit-them-on-the-nose American Medical Association. The very popular "secrets THEY don't want you to know" positioning you see used frequently these days—with, depending on what's being promoted, the IRS, FDA, medical establishment, Wall Street bankers, etc. as enemy of the people and suppressor of truth— owes great debt to John Brinkley. For quite some time, Brinkley succeeded with this positioning and, to the extreme frustration of Fishbein, the more Brinkley was publicly attacked, the more he made of it, and the more people sought him out and championed him and his 'cause'. Brinkley shrewdly understood that the public tended to root for the underdog, distrust The Establishment, and pay more attention to a champion of truth or justice under attack by powerful forces than to just about anyone or anything else.

This brings us to the subject of 'positioning', popularized as such by ad men Al Ries and Jack Trout, notably in the bestselling book of the

1980's, *Positioning: The Battle For The Mind*—but ably practiced decades before by Dr. Brinkley.

## *What Kind Of Hero Are You Known As?*

Brinkley positioned himself clearly and definitively as outlaw, renegade, and rogue; as crusader; as put-upon and oppressed underdog, only under assault because he dared to reveal truth, oppose the established powers that be, and fight for the common man. Because of this positioning, every public attack served to reinforce and strengthen his self-created status rather than to undermine it.

This is a very popular position among folk heroes. Consider: Robin Hood and Zorro. To some extent, Batman. A great deal of money has been made with this positioning too, by countless marketers, over time. You have certainly seen the persuasive pitchman Kevin Trudeau, in his much-aired television infomercials, selling his books of health cures, and of debt and money woe cures; with the first, positioning himself as a truth-teller daring to expose secrets the giant pharmaceutical companies and their toadies at the FDA wish to preserve, to such extent that they have attacked and persecuted him again and again; with the second, similarly positioning himself as the crusader fighting the rich, fat cat bankers, vile credit card companies and Wall Street tycoons as well as the FTC. Thus, if you Google him, and find the very long "rap sheet" of his battles with the FDA, FTC, states' attorney generals, his positioning is confirmed. Trudeau and Dr. Brinkley have much in common, but the scalpel. Trudeau is as blatant about all this as was Dr. Brinkley. But if you look alertly and closely at all the advertising and promotion circling

**FROM THE
BRINKLEY
BLUEPRINT:**
*Re-invention with
"new and improved."*

around you, now that you are alert for it, you will find this theme widely, if more demurely, used.

Fishbein's positioning is also a repeatedly effective staple. As noted above, Ralph Nader made himself famous—and relatively rich, although that's not common knowledge—with it. More recently, Michael Moore used the same positioning to establish himself in the film/documentary business, and to get very, very rich. Coincidentally—or not—Moore's first target was the same as Nader's: General Motors. In the media world, *Consumer Reports Magazine* and in its early years, *60 Minutes*. The men of *60 Minutes*, particularly Mike Wallace, made their reputations by ambushing and exposing John Brinkley-esque figures. The immensely popular radio and TV personality Dave Ramsey has positioned himself as a consumer advocate and common man champion, exposing how the banking and credit establishment entice and enslave. Until de-railed by sex scandal, Eliot Spitzer's rising star in politics, with the White House as ambition, was tied to his positioning as "the sheriff of Wall Street".

It shouldn't go unnoticed that Morris Fishbein was every bit as much of a self-promoter as his chosen adversary Dr. Brinkley, both relying on clear, definitive and dramatic positioning.

In his own ways, our own Dan Kennedy has consistently positioned himself as anti-establishment. Anti-brand, anti-image, anti-traditional advertising, with advertising agencies, the-bigger-they-are, the-dumber-they-are corporations and their pinhead executives, and tradition itself as his enemies. Chapter 1 of Dan's book, *No B.S. Direct Marketing*, stakes out this position concisely, if you'd like a sample of anti-conventional wisdom and anti-fads about management, with everyone from academic authorities and management and leadership gurus as foils. Insisting you must hold people ruthlessly accountable for productivity, and wring maximum profits from your business—the thesis of his book *No B.S. Ruthless Management of People and Profits.* Throughout his entire career, in marketing to professional speakers within the National Speakers Association's culture, in marketing to chiropractors and dentists, and in marketing to business owners and entrepreneurs generically, Dan has defied convention, taken contrarian positions, and challenged established traditions as well as institutions. This has not been accidental.

Within that frame, Dan has been abundantly and unequivocally clear about the fact that he is "all about the money", focused on profit, and intentional about extracting maximum profit from his every activity. This is one of the chief criticisms that has dogged him from market to market, and that fills the anti-Dan gossip online, but if those who've been influenced by his deliberate positioning encounter such criticism, it only serves to reinforce his position as advocate and teacher of enlightened self-interest and unabashed profiteering. His product brands are consistent—such as *No B.S.* and *Renegade Millionaire.* Even his choices of projects reinforce the outside the ordinary, anti-establishment, renegade positioning; as examples, he has chosen to co-author a book on selling with, and to promote as a sales consultant, the former Mayflower Madam, Sydney Barrows, a person with infamous past, and to co-author this book with me about a turn-of-the-century rogue at best, outright fraud at worst.

Dan has strived for clear, definitive and dramatic positioning throughout his 35-year career.

Have you?

**That is the million-dollar question** to be taken from this Chapter: how clear, definitive and dramatic is your positioning?

# 32

# Who Are You And What Do You Stand For?

*By Dan S. Kennedy*

**E**verything a blessing. This is a very difficult philosophical idea to own; yet it can be found in just about every exceptionally successful individual's performance. And, owning it directs an individual to certain ruminations, creative impulses and actions that the overwhelming majority of people never contemplate. As non-marketing, personal example, I can tell you that my divorce from Carla, after 22 years of marriage, felt like the end of the world to me at the time, and seemed final and irreversible, but our marriage now, post-divorce, is better than the previous one in many ways. It possible only because owning, to great extent, this philosophical concept directed my thinking and ultimately actions on a path most in the same situation would never consider.

There is that old story, which I'll abbreviate here: the young boy is given a horse for his birthday and all the villagers agreed he was a very fortunate young man, but the wise man said, "Wait. We'll see." Shortly thereafter, the boy was thrown from his horse, trampled, and had bones shattered in his legs. The villagers were horrified at the tragedy. The wise man said, "Wait. We'll see." War broke out, and many young men were drafted, sent to fight, and killed on the battlefield—but the injured young man could not go, and stayed behind, safe from harm. The villagers commented on this odd stroke of luck. And the wise man said...

The story can continue, ad infinitum.

So, consider the appearance of enemy or enemies, and their attacks. Would Sarah Palin have sold a million books were it not for the relentless, vicious, sarcastic and demeaning attacks waged against her nightly by cable news-talk media pundits on MSNBC and CNN, by popular liberal bloggers, and even in mainstream media? How many theater tickets for *Avatar* were sold thanks to the Catholic Church's denouncement of the movie? Would Ayn Rand have had the phenomenal success she had while alive and the enduring legacy of influence today had her novels not been publicly attacked by political and philosophical opponents? Certainly not. In fact, her first novel was dead in the water until the attacks began. These blessings of ardent, vocal and influential critics and sustained public attack can be found behind countless success stories.

It's very possible that John Brinkley would never have attracted as much attention (and money) without Morris Fishbein as he did with him attacking him at every turn. It's a certainty that Fishbein wouldn't have risen to his prominence without a John Brinkley. There are two linked lessons there for the astute marketer.

A story. In the late 1970's, I now forget the exact year, I returned home from my first National Speakers Association conference shocked and bitterly disappointed at discovering how little even the most celebrated 'big names'—and virtually everybody else there—knew about marketing themselves or marketing their authored products... when I had hoped to find people much smarter about this than I was, using strategies superior to those I'd cobbled together on my own. I immediately launched a newsletter titled *Marketing Your Services*, aimed at the NSA membership. At the start, I took no anti-establishment or critical position. I simply presented the facts about my background and success to-date, and offered the opportunity to participate in focused discussion of making the most money possible from a speaking-related business. This entailed, for example, always selling product from the platform and refusing to accept any engagement where prohibited from doing so; developing a powerful platform pitch; converting those one time buyers to on-going customers; taking control of the meeting environment and advance promotion to the client's conference attendees; and so on. I was honestly taken by surprise by the instant, vicious, intense and "loud" critical attacks from "name" old-timers, self-anointed speaking business protocol experts, ethicists, metaphysical spiritualists, and the association itself. I was quickly characterized as, written about and gossiped about as an idiot and a fool; a fraud and a liar; an unethical, money-grubbing Satan who would destroy all that was good and pure about the profession. **I found myself "an enemy of the state".**

**I relished the role.** I gladly accepted the gift given me and re-crafted my positioning to be all about challenging the quaint but antiquated traditions being clung to and defended; the remarkable ignorance about marketing, sales and business displayed; the selfish, fearful agenda of the old dogs, secretly eager to suppress young pups. I quoted the attacks on me chapter 'n verse. And when a Morris Fishbein opted to make it personal, I battled him publicly. My fledgling newsletter, that had received a very lukewarm initial response, suddenly skyrocketed in subscribers, thanks in large part to being 'the talk of the town'. I went on to very firmly—as Chip put it: clearly, definitively and dramatically—establish my position as controversial and, by many, reviled rogue of the industry, and I leveraged it to build up that newsletter, fill seminars, attract private clients, and many years' profit-taking from this small niche. As a matter of fact, my nine consecutive years appearing on Peter Lowe's SUCCESS events in 25 to 27 cities a year, with giant audiences, came as result of my visibility in the NSA world—and the gossip about me there. His curiosity was piqued, perhaps because he was a subject of considerable criticism, debate and dislikes himself. The consulting day he bought, calling me "cold", led to the 9 year relationship, and, for me, millions of dollars directly, more indirectly by elevation of status I would likely never have gotten otherwise. And if you wish to carry it further, my relationship with Bill Glazer and Glazer-Kennedy Insider's Circle™ exists because Bill attended one of those SUCCESS events—not of his own initiative, but as another attendee's guest. So, to my early "NSA enemies", thank y'all, very, very, very much.

## *Your Market Needs Clarity About You*

Controversy, criticism and adversaries aren't the only building blocks available for strong positioning. They're the ones John Brinkley chose—and had little choice but to choose, but they're not the only choices. The lesson here is not necessarily to encourage enemy attacks, but to *somehow* settle on and leverage some sort of very strong positioning, that is appealing to the target audience you want to attract.

My client, the Guthy-Renker Corporation, has made its Pro-Activ® brand the #1 acne treatment product line in America, out-selling all others. They have done so without attacking or deliberately inviting attacks from dermatologists—their product was developed by dermatologists. They've done it without engaging in public battle with the FDA as another client of mine did in the same category, before Guthy-Renker's entry; the doctor promoting a product called Acne-Statin, or ala Kevin Trudeau, mentioned by Chip. Instead, they've focused on being seen as the acne-fighting choice of Hollywood stars and popular music entertainers; on presenting overwhelming proof that their formula works; and on being America's #1 choice.

Probably because of their rather conservative corporate culture, they have avoided picking public fights, bloody combat with competitors or serious controversy, although I can tell you from direct, personal knowledge, all such ideas are periodically re-visited and considered, as the competitive landscape changes, as the internet provides an increasingly expansive and active opportunity for negative gossip and complaining, and as sales ebb and flow. Before the end of this brand's story is written, you may yet see some Brinkley-ish positioning. But up until now, no. At present, their positioning is (a) as the hip, in vogue, popular product *everybody* who's anybody or knows anything is using, so why aren't you?—get with it! ... and (b) as the science-based, inarguably proven product that actually works. In many ways, they are The Establishment, fighting to stay relevant, and fighting off up-start competitors. The fact that this approach has built, from zero, a billion dollar brand, and continues to work, speaks volumes about your having options in positioning, but also about the critical importance of positioning.

**FAILING TO CONTROL YOUR POSITIONING GUARANTEES SOMEONE ELSE WILL.**

The last thing I'd like to say here about the subject is: failing to strategically, purposefully and aggressively craft and control your positioning just about guarantees someone will do it for you. Someone else will position you in the mind of the marketplace, and it will probably be somebody who doesn't have your best interests at heart. You need to accept this responsibility and make it a priority. It's best to choose sustainable positioning that is reasonably congruent with who you really are and what you really stand for, and to then take the greatest care not to be "found out" as at odds with it.

It's interesting that Charlie Sheen's success as one of the most successful, most popular, and highest paid TV sit-com stars has held up over years despite his much publicized adventures with hookers, marital discord, arrests, etc., presumably because his character in *Two And A Half Man* was created with his off-screen realities in mind, and whatever his latest real life mess is, it's neither shock or disappointment to his fans. If anything, it reinforces positioning that has been accepted. Revelations of Tiger Woods' infamous dalliances with 14 or 16 or 18 different women, from pancake house waitress to porn star, while married quickly stripped away his endorsement contracts, corporate sponsors and commercial value, and left him in a very, very deep hole to climb out of, over time, at great cost, if he is ever to restore his once brilliant luster—precisely because the antics were in hair-raising contradiction to his positioning.

Tiger made sure we saw photos and video of him and happy family, holding hands affectionately with his wife, rushing over to her and the kids after a victory. He was also positioned as an impossibly cool, calm, collected person imbued with admirable self-discipline and super-human powers of focus and concentration. He was presented as an upstanding citizen surrounded by a cast of corporate characters like leading financial services firms, auto brands, and energy drinks—in the tradition of preceding clean-cut, All-American-boy type golf personalities like Arnold Palmer. The public was ill-prepared to discover he's more John Daly than Arnie, utterly absent control over his worst impulses, ultimately copping to addiction, a serial philanderer and liar to all; wife, mistresses, media. The actions are one thing; the inconsistency with positioning, another.

Ultimately, your clientele and constituency wants to know who you are and what you stand for, then see that you are who you say you are, and that you do stand for what you say you do. Failure at this strips enormously popular politicians of all their power and sends them packing, in ignominy. Again and again, over and over. A lesson never learned by the next arrogant megalomaniac to come along, believing he is so charismatic or dynamic he can get away with such fundamental incongruity between positioning and performance. Failure at this topples mighty product and business brands, sometimes with dizzying speed. Failure at this wastes millions of dollars of advertising extolling virtues of products, companies or individuals quickly discovered by their customers to be figments of ad men's imaginations.

Positioning is a vitally important strategy, producing an enormously valuable yet very vulnerable asset.

# PRINCIPLE #19

## CREATIVELY RESPONDING TO
# SETBACKS

# Re-Invention On A Grand Scale

### By Chip Kessler

The John Brinkley Money Machine ultimately collapsed and disintegrated, as most frauds usually do. There was destruction wrought by outside forces as well as significant self-destruction, wrought by egotism and arrogance, waging too many wars on too many fronts with too-powerful of opponents, poor judgment, wildly profligate spending. Brinkley's character flaws far outweighed his character strengths. But when you consider how long John Brinkley did perpetuate an expansive, infamous, multi, multi-million dollar (in inflation adjusted dollars, perhaps a billion dollar) marketing operation… more than once virtually destroyed but then rising from ashes as a more powerful phoenix… **you have to marvel at the man's resilience and durability. And you should wonder, what is it testament to?**

For one thing, credit goes to the evergreen, universal, and deeply emotional nature of the big ideas on which is product, propositions, positioning and promises were based, and to his genius in settling on those ideas. One can't ignore that a "fountain of youth" is secretly wished for by just about everybody (thus something people want to believe in), and something many are secretly, quietly or openly seeking. Today, at extremes, there are people selling and people buying "cryogenics"—having themselves or at least their heads fast-frozen upon death and kept in a state of suspended animation until some future time when their disease or aging itself is cured, they can be thawed, pull the tarp off their sports car and resume picking up girls! John Brinkley would love the cryogenics business. "Anti-aging" has become an industry, and "anti-aging medicine" a legitimized sub-set of the medical profession. Pharmaceutical drugs very specifically addressing the need that Dr. Brinkley's goat glands transplants purported to cure are among the most popular, profitable drugs, and are openly advertised in every media. Their less-legitimate herbal and nutrition cousins are sold by the millions, predominately via online marketing, but also from health food store and drugstore shelves. One of the most popular of these concoctions, by the way, is "Horny Goat Weed", a nutritional supplement that promises sexual vitality, and credits the same source or inspiration, as did Brinkley's surgery. The fastest growth segment of the skin care industry is anti-aging serums and creams and potions, commanding remarkably high prices. All around us, an aging population—the front line of boomers hit 65 in 2010, and 30-million Americans will add themselves to the Social Security rolls between now and 2020, and all around us, a youth-obsessed culture. Selling some made-believable fountain of youth is going to produce fountains of money for some time to come.

Still, Brinkley's choice of product and subject matter, and his prowess and daring as a promoter notwithstanding, there is another ingredient, it a character strength, that contributed enormously to his success as long as it lasted. Simply put, John Brinkley refused to lose.

## *How Do You Vanquish The Opponent Who Refuses To Lose?*

There is a sports cliché that I became very familiar with during my broadcasting career—*this game will go to the team that wants it the most.* It's a time-honored cliché because it embodies a great deal of truth. However, it's my observation that more close games and extremely competitive match-ups are decided by one competitor's refusal to lose than by desire to win.

To start off with, refusing to lose is much easier said than done. After all, everyone quits at something in life, maybe even several something's through time ... how about you? We quit a class we started because we didn't like the instructor or we suddenly decided that we had more important things to do on Tuesday and Thursday nights than sit for two hours and learn about whatever it was we enrolled in the class to learn in the first place. Maybe you quit taking guitar lessons? Perhaps it was a job? Whatever it was—you quit! In all likelihood, quitting the guitar or some obscure night class isn't going to ruin your life. Maybe not even change it in any significant way. Napoleon Hill once commented that quitting some thing harmed few, but quitting many things made a habit that harmed many. It's worth contemplating how many things you quit and give up on or start but don't follow-through on in your business. We don't get paid for the things we start; only for those we complete.

John R. Brinkley had every reason to quit before he ever got started. Growing up poor in some out-of-the-way Western North Carolina mountain town didn't give him any obvious foundation for fame and fortune. We can assume that many others born the same week he was, in the same geographic area he was, raised in the same kind of poverty he was, never so much as imagined anything better for themselves, and stayed put where they were rooted. Brinkley used the poverty he faced as a youth as motivation to break away from what surrounded him, and to seek a better life. And Brinkley's definition of a better life included enough money to buy whatever he wanted at the time, whether in any given moment it was a big new car, an exciting vacation, or things like hospitals or radio stations. He became a visionary who acted on his ideas and ambitions, and saw them through, even against considerable odds and stiff opposition.

As Brinkley progressed from minor league medicine show pitchman to famous healer attracting patients from all over the country to firebrand personality to enemy of the state, he encountered times when everything went awry—when his fast pace on his progressive path suddenly led off a cliff. Brinkley crashed more than once. And in every such instance, he…

*…re-invented himself.*

As example, when his method was discredited, and oddly, at the same time commoditized, it was the same Dr. John R. Brinkley who emerged, with a *new* technique for combating the same problem of male impotence. Long before Proctor & Gamble discovered the **power of adding three words** to their laundry detergent packages and advertising every 3 to 4 months, John Brinkley embraced the concept of: *new and improved…* a daring contradiction in terms! If it is improved, it must actually be old and improved. If it is new, it can't be improved; there was nothing to improve. No matter. In other words, J.R. Brinkley had done it again! He had "gone back to the drawing board" and employed his unmatched genius as a medical scientist combined with resolute determination, and had discovered an even better solution than before! On that foundation, a new and improved Dr. Brinkley stepped forward, again *the* leader in his field. (If you do not see the Brinkley blueprint there, that you can use anytime your methods have been discredited or competitively positioned as out-dated, or your marketing has gone stale, you need to have your eyes checked promptly!)

In this case, Brinkley's "new and improved" was presented by announcement that Doctor John R. Brinkley was no longer calling on male goats to be the source of restoring a man's sexual prowess—despite his long-standing promotion of that method. Rather, he had developed an entirely new surgical procedure that would deliver superior, entirely reliable results to the sex-starved male. What was this breakthrough with a knife and scalpel? Ah this is another Brinkley marketing gem to make note of: *it was too complicated to go into great detail about only that it had something to do with the dismal relationship (at least before letting the doctor operate on you) between the male organ/testicles and the epididymus.* Here J.R. Brinkley's response led the questioner into a confusing array of medical teachings and details best left to those trained to comprehend such complex information. In other words, *take my word for it.*

This change in surgical technique also led John R. Brinkley to another part of the male body, which led him to the cause of many a man's health problems: the prostate. About this, the Brinkley marketing machine went to work, on a grand scale, mailing new information to accumulated, yet unconverted prospective patients as well as newly interested men, revealing the evils imbedded within an unhealthy prostate, and presenting the cure uniquely available from Dr. Brinkley. He had found new life with a new enemy: the prostate.

In this re-invention, Brinkley also focused more of his energies on more affluent patients. His marketing literature listed the new and improved, best option as the one recommended for men who owned *the finest automobiles ... the finest homes ... the best horses ... best diamonds ... the best works of art.* Brinkley also reportedly marketed his prostate procedure as featuring

**HIGH VALUE QUESTION:** *when you suffer a setback,* HOW MANY WAYS *do you creatively and simultaneously respond?*

the Compound Technique, the Rock of Gibraltar of Dr. Brinkley's work! And, after undergoing the procedure, each patient was charged an additional $100.00 for six bottles of Brinkley's "Formula 1020" to be injected systematically after the patient returned home. The "formula" was the doctor's personal, proprietary creation to stimulate the rejuvenated prostate back to good health.

Combined, John Brinkley responded to the challenge to his methods that might have left a lesser man wounded and paralyzed with three proactive measures: he came forward with a new and improved product/solution for the need he had been so successfully exploiting; he simultaneously premiered a product for another, related need, for which an array of new and additional beneficial promises could be advanced; and he focused his energies on mining the least price resistant segment of his market. **This begs the question: *when you suffer a setback in your business, how many ways do you creatively and simultaneously respond?***

Each time that Brinkley got knocked down, he not only rose up and re-invented himself, but he upped the ante. He came back on an even bigger scale than he had operated before. He positioned each comeback not as a return, but as a grand and glorious accomplishment. He was never content just to get back in the game after injury—he sought to change the game!

As example, when John Brinkley was basically driven out of Kansas, and emerged in Del Rio, Texas, he relied on his greatest media discovery—radio—for his re-birth. But he didn't settle for merely replicating what he had done before.

The new and improved communications weapon he built across the Texas boarder, radio station XERA in Mexican town of Villa Acuna, beyond reach of the U.S. government regulators, was built to dwarf broadcasting stations in the U.S., quickly growing (with the consent of the Mexican government) first to 150,000 watts then to 500,000 watts to, finally, 1,000,000 watts ... an unheard of radio signal strength. As Pope Brock reports in *Charlatan*, with one million watts, the voice of Dr. John R. Brinkley was now heard in every state in the union, plus the far off reaches of Alaska (many years before it became a state) and several foreign countries. With this reach, John Brinkley not only made himself a bigger personality and force of marketing than ever before, but was able to be a "star-maker" for others he built products for and businesses around, notably including a fabulously successful female pitchwoman, Rose Dawn. With Rose, remedies for every imaginable ailment of far lower cost than Brinkley's surgeries were sold to the huge numbers of listeners not ready or able to undergo the knife. To this end, Dr. Brinkley created and controlled his own competition. Once started down the path of diversification, Brinkley did not stop simply with creating a small stable of other pitch-persons and product lines, and in the Home Study Course, we discuss some of the other diversification maneuvers he took during this time in Texas and south of the border.

To the frustration of his critics and enemies, and delight of the public, it seemed, for a lengthy span of time, impossible to make Dr. John Brinkley go away. Each time it appeared he might fade away to distant memory, he re-appeared, re-invented, with bigger ideas, bolder marketing messages, and more aggressive marketing than before. This may be a hallmark of the super-entrepreneur, this unique trait of always falling forward.

# ③④

# Two Judges

### By Dan S. Kennedy

**T**here are only two judges whose judgments really matter, in deciding the outcomes in a person's life: his, and that of the audience or market that supports him, or at some point, deserts him. High achievers learn to ignore all other judges and their verdicts. Most people instead accept just about any judge who presents himself as having authority over them, and accept just about any verdict handed down. Defiance is a very powerful force—so much so, I'm slowly working on an entire book about it. In Brinkley, we find an *extremely* defiant individual.

Frank Sinatra was twice pronounced a living "thing of the past" during his career, dropped by his record labels, virtually black-listed from television, judged by all those who judge such things as *old news*. In one instance, Sinatra had to raise capital and create his own record company because not a single established entity would agree to release a Sinatra album. That company became the very successful Capitol Records, ultimately sold for a small fortune. And, of course, Sinatra went on to a few more decades of top-of-the-heap success. Dead, he brings in more money than a long, long, long list of living recording artists and will most certainly outlast many for whom fame proves fleeting. In one recent month, I found Sinatra singing in three different newly released movies and two different TV commercials, and I'm confident no other artist, living or dead, had the same exposure. While his successive comebacks may be more epic than many, America is the land of comebacks—for entertainers, politicians, product brands, companies and others, whether tarred by scandal or merely prematurely discarded as a thing of the past. The best rise up, as John Brinkley did, bigger, bolder, badder than before.

Then there are those who appear to rival cats for number of lives. Cher leaps to mind, as queen of re-invention and re-incarnation. Clint Eastwood made un-bankable as leading man and action hero by age re-invented himself as a highly respected, award winning director with a string of both critically acclaimed and very profitable movies to his credit. Then by financing, creating and producing his own movies, he was able to cast himself in heroic roles he never would have been given by 'outsiders', and win critical acclaim and at the box office with a couple of those times at bat as well. The entire genre of comic book super-heroes and the comic book industry had a Golden Age, then faded in prominence all the way to irrelevance and near extinction, but has enjoyed re-birth and renaissance, to point of several of the biggest blockbuster movie hits of recent years featuring caped crusaders from the pages of comic books, and Disney recently investing billions in acquiring Marvel Entertainment. Whether an individual or an entire industry, re-invention is always possible, periodically if not cyclically necessary and is woven into American culture.

Even concepts get re-invented and gain whole new lives. The Survivor-style reality show is, in essence, the game show re-invented. The immensely popular American Idol is a reincarnation of talent competition shows dating all the way back to radio, pre-dating television, including very famous predecessors like Ted Mack's Amateur Hour. Walt Disney famously re-imagined and re-invented the ordinary amusement park. In one, you can visit a dozen different countries complete with marvelously authentic landmarks, town squares, shops, restaurants and staff imported from the actual countries. This is a transplant and re-invention of the once immensely popular different-country-every-day tours of Europe, immortalized in the move titled 'If It's Tuesday, It Must Be Belgium'. The most daring, very Brinkley-ish business reinvention I love making fun of is Subway® from fast-food alternative to weight loss program, with Jared. This, a most preposterous idea that has improbably survived for more than ten years.

The temptation to procrastinate about re-invention is natural and significant. Consequently, re-invention occurs mostly as it did for John Brinkley: under extreme duress, or with people launching entirely new businesses in tired industries, like Disney, or Howard Schultz with coffee shops, or a business I advise, Kennedy's All-American Barber Clubs, which you can see at KennedysBarberClub.com. However, most business owners could benefit greatly by voluntarily and proactively re-inventing in advance of need, or least not living in denial at early indications of evolving need.

Whatever else he was, good, bad, opportunistic, predatory, worse, one thing that John Brinkley definitely was might best be described as creatively, ambitiously and aggressively resilient. Whenever he was uprooted and had to re-establish his business or saw a pitch wearing out or had a marketing tool or opportunity forcibly taken away from him, he hardly slowed in re-inventing on an even more ambitious scale and promoting in an even more aggressive way.

He attacked the market on multiple fronts, with multiple methods. He embodied the behavioral principle my late friend Jim Rohn taught as "the Principle of MASSIVE Action." In this alone, John Brinkley is worthy of study—and of asking: how do you measure up?

# PRINCIPLE #20

### RELENTLESS
# FOLLOW-UP

# PRINCIPLE #21

### PERFECTING A
# SYSTEM

# 35

# Dogged Pursuit

## By Chip Kessler

**B**ehind all the bombast and hype and noise making, and underneath the exceptionally effective advertising and marketing, and innovative, groundbreaking use of media, there was a relatively dull and boring, methodical and pedantic component of the Brinkley blueprint for success, un-remarked upon by the media and under-appreciated by observers.

**Having built successful businesses of my own and consulted with many, I've found that, almost without exception, there is at least one, often several inglorious and inherently uninteresting key components, that must be put in place and kept functioning well, that make all the difference between success and failure.** In every case, there are more visible and more exciting moving parts, but without the virtually invisible or unappreciated key components, all the power of all the others would be greatly de-valued. As a consultant, I think identifying these and insuring they are in good working order is important.

In the case of John Brinkley, there was a great deal that was very visible. His dynamic personality, his outrageous but irresistible proposition, his use of media, and much more. But it all might have been for naught without an unheralded factor. His business might have been economically unsustainable absent this component.

The Brinkley Marketing & Money Machine had, as one if its most important cogs, *relentless follow-up*.

Dr. Brinkley did not take the simplistic approach of advertising simply to bring patients through the door of an office. He was in the business of lead generation. In advertisements, circulars, direct-mail, and on his radio programs, Brinkley almost always offered some sort of pamphlet, booklet, or book, sometimes free, sometimes for some small payment, in order to secure the names and addresses of as many interested—or at least curious—people as possible for each dollar spent in advertising. Then, after a person had raised his hand, a series of follow-up pieces arrived in his mailbox. If you are a student of Dan Kennedy's, and familiar with his basic letter sequence model, this will strike a familiar chord.

In *Charlatan,* author Pope Brock describes one of Dr. Brinkley's sequences thusly:

> *Anyone who replied, however idly, to one of his flyers was peppered with finely tuned follow-ups. Their tone was pleasant the first two or three times. Then ...****Dr. Brinkley's Fourth Follow-up Correspondence****: (read, in part:)*

> Is the joke on me?

> Your request for more literature led me to believe you were intending to come and see me and I sent it gladly.

You have not made an appointment and I'm wondering if you were just "kidding" me … If you have no intention of coming to see me just say so and there will be no hard feelings.

Honesty is always the best policy.

### *Then, Dr. Brinkley's Fifth Follow-up Correspondence:*

Just what kind of fellow are you?

You wrote to us for information regarding our work and we sent it to you … Now after we have sent you literature and have written you … we can't even hear from you.

### *Dr. Brinkley's Sixth Follow-up Correspondence:*

This is your final notice … Do not ask for one second's extension. It will not be granted.

Let's examine the above follow-ups for a few moments.

➤ All of Brinkley's last three follow-ups put the reader on the immediate defensive via an accusatory tone

➤ Two of the three (number four along with number five) begin with a headline that clearly makes the reader understand that Brinkley is dumbfounded at the lack of action on their part

➤ All three state a definite call to action, whether it's to write back and tell Dr. Brinkley that you are no longer interested or now wish to make an appointment to come see him

> The final follow-up (number six in his sequence) features Brinkley's brand of take-away selling stating in no uncertain terms that the time to stop pussyfooting around is now, how you better not let this opportunity pass you by, then suddenly have an attack of remorse and come begging for another chance at seeing the doctor for his services because it won't even be considered

> All three of these notices clearly imply that Dr. John R. Brinkley's time is very valuable and that he is an extremely busy man … so how dare you infer early on that you were interested in his services and now are leaving him hanging in limbo waiting for you to respond

> The first and second follow-ups listed (numbers four and five in his sequence) imply that you are playing fast and loose ("honesty is the best policy") with the Doctor's good graces since you are not even willing to let him know that you're no longer interested - a challenge to your integrity, and by implication, reinforcement of his

> All three final communications specifically pinpoint and state the fact that it was you that contacted him wanting to know more about what Dr. Brinkley had to offer, he did not knock on your door uninvited, so it's expected of you to now follow through

Am I reading more into these than you did? You have to consider the time in which these letters were used, a time when civility and courtesy was the norm, and such a confrontational tone—a bill collector's tone—

was rarely encountered, and certainly not in letters from somebody you didn't know and had no relationship with. Most people undoubtedly re-read each letter a second time, perhaps more, and asked themselves: what does he mean by this? They read meaning into it, between the lines, as I did. This was also a time when honesty, integrity, proper behavior mattered, so taking the time of the doctor, asking for information from him did carry some obligation.

The shift in tone from the first few friendly, gentle follow-up pieces (not quoted here) to these sterner, more authoritative and somewhat annoyed pieces suggests a determination by Brinkley that, after a certain amount of follow-up was ignored, he had nothing to lose by switching from selling to chastisement and intimidation.

While peoples' attitudes are different today, this same model, including the change in tone, still works in a great many situations. Dan Kennedy has been using and teaching it since the late 1970's but continues relying on it today. The only significant difference I can see between this sequence and others by Dr. Brinkley that I examined, and the sequences used by Dan and his clients now, is that Dan has added a definite stated deadline, that can be counted down to, and referred to in the copy, while Brinkley relied on a more general sense of urgency and limited supply. Otherwise, no discernible difference, thus this is a strategy that has stood the test of time!

John Brinkley not only employed these linked sequences for follow-up, with four, six, eight, even a dozen letters, each mentioning the preceding one, but he also routinely barraged his entire list of accumulated prospects who had not arranged appointments with separate mailings whenever he had a new and improved procedure, exceptionally interesting patient's success story, hospital re-location, or other "news" to convey. Keep in mind, this was all occurring long before computers and databases, and easy, quick, inexpensive preparation and printing of materials, so every direct-mail campaign had to be a "project", and keeping track of which prospects should get Letter #3 and which were ready for Letter #6 no simple matter. Sticking with this kind of organized, timed, multi-step follow-up required considerable discipline and commitment, considerable investment, and an understanding of its importance. Even with modern technology and convenience, most business owners fail this test today!

# 36

# Do YOU Have A System For Success?

*By Dan S. Kennedy*

I'm a very serious student of advertising and marketing history, so I'm pretty much aware that nobody's inventing anything, and just how valuable it can be to go back in time, to be inspired by and borrow from guys like John Brinkley. My saying is: there's old in the gold.

As example, there are a lot of ways to accuse a prospect of being foolish or stupid or negligent by not responding. I have often used the letter from "J. Squirrel", written by a squirrel, headlined "Are Ya Nuts?", with a little bag of peanuts attached or enclosed. This softens the blow a bit, but the point is exactly the same as Brinkley's "Just What Kind Of Fellow Are You?" I have also glued a little compass onto the top of an "Are you Lost?" letter, which then sarcastically suggests the reader may have been lost in the woods for the past three weeks or been unable to find his way to the post office to mail back his response.

I found this approach before I found John Brinkley's work, but I did find it in examples from other marketers' of Brinkley's era. I went back in time to the 1930's to borrow a concept I used in 1980—and still use—to make money.

The sequence, and increasingly stern, frustrated or annoyed tone in each successive step, is something I borrowed from the dunning letter sequences I got from the many collection agencies, banks and others I owed money to at one very bad time. I noticed that this was a common ingredient in all of them. Research has shown me its use by Brinkley, by the great ad man Robert Collier, by ministers seeking donations, all the way back into the 1920's. It is, as Chip noted, a tested and proven and reliable strategy.

In the Home Study Course that is an extension of this book, we've included about 100 pages or so of John Brinkley letters, marketing materials, radio shows, etc., all worthy of study—and borrowing from. Which you can do with impunity. Dr. Brinkley and his wife are both departed.

## From The Brinkley Blueprint: The Closed Loop

As a copywriter, I'm naturally fascinated by and focused on the copy itself. The themes, the ideas, the words used, the style and tone. But I know better than to pay attention only to this, the glamorous side of things, but ignore the structure. The exciting view of the city and the bay seen from the 30th floor balcony is possible because of ugly metal girders and cement foundations. Structure matters. Brinkley was ahead of his time in this regard. Few marketers of his time that I've researched were as sophisticated in capturing prospects and then engaging in complex, multi-step, timed follow-up. As Chip noted, it's not easy to get a business owner committed to it today, let alone at a time entirely without any automation or other technology. Brinkley recognized that there was value buried deep in his leads, to be mined with diligent digging. Presumably he realized he could not invest as heavily in advertising, publicity, promotion and grandiose facilities as he needed to if he was to totally dominate the market and make himself famous if he wasted any of that value. This closed-loop thinking... out-spend everyone else in creating fame and generating leads and then diligently, thoroughly squeeze every drop of value from those leads so you can afford to out-spend everyone else... is very much to his credit. I find opposite thinking in most entrepreneurs now and can only assume Brinkley's thinking was foreign to everyone then.

It's fun for most people to do the topside stuff. To be their own John Brinkley. To create clever advertising and exciting promotions, to sell, to perform their service. But without giving just attention to the bottom-side stuff, everything done up top is partly if not wholly wasted. My book *No B.S. Ruthless Management of People and Profits* is about bottom-side matters. I wrote it for the very reason that most businesspeople neglect such matters in favor of those up top, which are more fun, less stressful; require less discipline and diligence.

When you read about John Brinkley, you'll think he was a "loose cannon". In many respects, you're right. He was. To the point of making some very impulsive and ill-advised decisions. Even making news as a drunk, in violent altercations. He was obviously unrestrained by either personal commitment to honesty or by the law. He sometimes spent money he did not have, sometimes in foolish ways. He made a lot of trouble for himself unnecessarily. You will take notice of all these flaws. You'll also certainly acknowledge that he was a brilliant marketer and promoter, persuasive salesman and masterful communicator, and visionary entrepreneur. But in all of that don't miss something important revealed by the sophistication of his follow-up systems and his strict implementation of them: he brought an engineer's organized thoughtfulness to making his marketing a well-designed process, rather than a bunch of random acts. There was system at work here, from start to finish; from formula for every radio broadcast; to precisely choreographed welcoming and handling of patients; to follow-up with leads.

I have often observed and taught that, in in-depth analysis, all wealth can be traced to systems. If your income is less than you'd like, it's a safe assumption that are significant system flaws in your business and business life. As erratic as John Brinkley might have been as an individual, he created, installed and adhered to systems in his business.

# BONUSES

# Samuel Griffith Brinkley
# & making the most of what you've got

*By Chip Kessler*

**S**amuel Griffith Brinkley was a cousin of Dr. Brinkley's. Samuel Griffith Brinkley was born in the Toe River Valley region of Mitchell County, North Carolina on September 21, 1850 and died on December 13, 1929. While he certainly never achieved the fame or infamy of his distant cousin, he did mimic the self-promotional approach to making a living.

As his picture tells you in an instant, it wasn't very hard at all to discover what Sam Brinkley's most recognizable feature was! Yet from a marketing perspective, having or possessing something such as Brinkley's remarkable beard, and being able to use it to your best advantage and make it pay are two different things altogether.

How many people possess some asset—a talent, a skill, an eccentricity, an interest or passion, something—they never recognize as potentially valuable, or never develop the confidence, initiative and promotional know-how to exploit? It's worth asking yourself if you have latent assets that might be exploited.

In the case of Sam Brinkley, that asset was his beard. A beard that, at its greatest length, extended from his face down his chest, stomach, legs and feet until it hit the floor and then dragged some three inches on the floor. At its longest, his beard was said to have grown to over six feet in length.

SAM G. BRINKLEY
Buladean, N. C.
Longest Bearded Man in the World
Beard - 5 ft. 5 in.

For Sam Brinkley, it became his calling card in life and allowed him to travel the country, visit parts of the world and to at one point even have a face-to-face (or in this particular case, a beard-to-beard) meeting with the King of England.

During the 79 years that the long-bearded Brinkley roamed the earth, he lived a remarkable life due to the one unique and special characteristic that set him apart from other men at the time and made him instantly recognizable to all who knew him or would get to meet him.

The legend is that Brinkley, like a great many men of his day, was clean shaven until he was 26 years old, though young Sam was paying a price for his smooth appearance because he was forced to use a razor two or three times a day due to his unusually heavy facial growth of whiskers. It was enough aggravation to make a man want to shed the chore of shaving forever. And thus a celebrity was born!

His face, now free of a razor, quickly transformed itself. While 99.9% of men who stopped shaving would see a thick, bushy and somewhat lengthy beard appear, Sam Brinkley's beard kept growing and growing and growing, to his outrageous length. When people saw him, they stopped in their tracks, asked him questions if they could, and told everyone they knew about the strange fellow with the remarkably long beard they'd encountered.

Everyone else wondered if such a man really existed, and if so, where could they see him for themselves?

"I can honestly say that I gasped after seeing a picture of my great-great-grandfather for the very first time," admits Deborah Brinkley Kessler. "The kind of beard he had wasn't anything you would run across, even back in his time. If nothing else, it had to have made him a very memorable character to everyone he came into contact with and the kind of person that once you saw him or met him, you weren't soon going to forget."

Despite all the notoriety and local fame the facial hair brought him, Brinkley was becoming more and more inconvenienced having to lug around his vast beard. One can only imagine the mere chore of walking to and fro and having to shuffle your feet in such a way as to not trip over the thing!

"My mother would talk about how neat and clean my great-grandfather was," explains James Brinkley. "She said he was the kind of man who never liked to get any dirt or mud on his clothes or his shoes even though the streets back in his time weren't paved. So I'm sure that he wanted to keep his beard as neat and clean as he possibly could."

One day Sam Brinkley came up with the solution. He had a special cloth bag made that enabled him to roll his beard up (just like a person would roll up a piece of carpet) and place it into the sack, which was on a string worn around his neck. Brinkley then tucked the bag (with its hairy contents) inside his shirt against his chest. As a result, people he'd encounter would no longer see Sam Brinkley walking around "hanging out" so to speak, but instead saw only the facial growth and a tad more underneath his chin. The remainder of the Brinkley legendary beard would now be left up to a person's imagination. Or so Samuel Griffith Brinkley thought.

But, faced with wanting to see something and in turn being denied the very opportunity, a person's wants and desires always triumph— including triumph over courtesy. A marketer might label this as his or her dream scenario: causing a prospective client, customer or patient to get so emotionally charged up that prospect will stop at nothing to get what they want from you.

True to form of wanting what they can't have, despite the large majority of his beard now being tucked away from a person's eyesight, men and women weren't content with just a portion of the Sam Brinkley "experience." Accordingly, they'd come up to Sam wherever he might be at the time, and ask him to take his full beard out in order for them to gaze upon it.

Grasping the peoples' desire to view his most import asset, the "Brinkley" in Sam came to the forefront. For if there was something that the people wanted, and a Brinkley was involved, then he was going to figure out a way and means to give them what they desired.

Naturally, however, what they desired would come at a price, as Sam decided:

*"Why let people see something for free when you can charge them for the privilege?"*

"The story was that he would charge a person ten cents to then have him unroll his beard and take a look at it," says James Brinkley of his great-grandfather. "The fee was twenty five cents to show it to a group. You have to give him credit for sensing a business opportunity and then capitalizing on it."

And that he did ... and then some.

True to Brinkley form, if you could earn some many via one avenue (charge a dime or a quarter in some cases for "the great beard reveal") then there had to be a way to further take advantage of this most memorable attribute. Next, he had picture-postcards printed up featuring him and his beard in all its glory, Sam standing erect and the growth all rolled out to the floor. Now a person could:

1. Pay a dime (or the group rate of a quarter) for the opportunity to watch the beard unfurl

2. Pay an additional sum to purchase one or several of Sam Brinkley's postcards

The postcard angle was an exceptionally shrewd one from a marketing perspective, for not only did Sam have a second item to sell but once the postcard was bought the person who purchased it was sure to show it around to their family, relatives and friends. The result: more and more people became familiar with one Samuel Griffith Brinkley and would seek him out and then pay for the opportunity to see his beard.

I am guessing that you don't possess a beard that falls to the ground plus three inches, however, chances are you have "something" you can tie yourself to and use as a hook to create more interest in what you are offering. And the use of 'personal attributes" has certainly not been unique to Samuel Brinkley. Famous artist Leroy Nieman's flamboyant mustache served quite effectively as his distinctive trademark. Elvis grew long sideburns before they became popular—and favored dramatic costumes on stage. The Beatles' mop-top haircuts were initially unique. Donald Trump's hair is an unending topic of conversation and target of comedians.

Country singer Crystal Gayle's hair rivals Samuel Brinkley's beard in length. Jimmy Durante and Bob Hope made much of their noses, Leno of his chin, and, well, who isn't very much aware of Dolly Parton's attention-getters. Then there's wardrobe. Michael Jackson's glove. Larry King's suspenders. The make-up and costumes created by Gene Simmons for KISS. As iconic images go, Dan Kennedy in business suit perched upon the giant albino bull is well known to hundreds of thousands of business owners, as is the "No B.S." philosophy it symbolizes. Dr. Brinkley was, of course, even more closely identified with the goat than Dan is with the "No B.S." bull!

One of the lessons of Samuel Brinkley's source of prosperity and fame is that even small things can be leveraged in big ways. Many people sadly sell themselves short, believing they lack anything special enough to turn into fame and fortune. But attention can be commanded, fascination fostered, and opportunities made possible with even the most ordinary of things, presented as important. For example, Dan Kennedy frequently remarks that most of his customers are amazed at his long-held habit of reading a book a day. People constantly expressed curiosity at how he could accomplish such a feat.

In a moment of candor, Dan shared the secret with Glazer-Kennedy Insider Circle™ members—he said:

*"First you select a book to read, next you find a quiet spot to sit down, and then you open the book to the first page and you begin to read it, and keep reading, and before you know it, you have read the book!"*

Obviously, there's a bit more to it. Dan is an accomplished speed-reader who has trained himself to also achieve an exceptionally high level of comprehension. But the point here is that when Dan mentions this habit and this ability, it captured peoples' curiosity and imagination. As speed-readers go, he's far surpassed by Howard Berg, recognized by Guinness Book of World Records as the world's fastest reader. That status has consistently brought the media to Howard, and given him millions of dollars of useful publicity. In December of 2009, Howard appeared on a Fox News program for several consecutive days, reading the Senate's health care reform bill. Howard has parlayed this one skill and "claim to fame" into a successful career spanning decades as author, speaker, corporate trainer, as well as profitable associations with educational organizations, even appearances in television commercials. In reality, the skill Dan has that most impresses Glazer-Kennedy Insider's Circle™ Members is his unending ability to bring new ideas, information, insights and provocative examples from a wide diversity of industries and people—this made possible, in large part, by his vaunted ability to read more and process more information than any ten people.

While Sam Brinkley's reading ability and habits wasn't enough to land him a spot as a feature performer in the circus, his beard did the trick. Always on the lookout for "unusual" talent and attractions, the Barnum and Bailey circus got wind of the man in North Carolina with the most unique physical characteristic: the world's longest beard. Once he began touring with the show, thousands of people from different parts of the country became aware of Samuel Griffith Brinkley and his outrageous beard.

Brinkley also visited Canada with the circus. While there, the current reigning monarch King Edward VII of Great Brittan was visiting this part of the British Empire. Sporting a robust growth of facial hair himself, the king was anxious to meet Sam Brinkley. During their visit, the king gave Brinkley a photo of himself and autographed it for good measure. We can assume that Sam presented King Edward with one of his picture postcards in order to return the favor!

Sam Brinkley also toured with the famous Buffalo Bill Wild West Show, and made paid personal appearances at all manner of other events.

As mentioned earlier in this chapter, Samuel Griffith Brinkley died on December 13, 1929. He's buried in his native Western North Carolina soil near the town of Buladean.

In recognition of the power of his beard as trademark, the same photo of Samuel Brinkley and his beard that graced his famous postcard is engraved on his granite gravestone.

I suppose that most would consider Samuel Brinkley, his beard, and his life of little importance. But I view it as an inspiring tale of a man who made much of little, who proved the power of self-promotion. If ol' Sam Brinkley can create a lifelong career, make a good living, and travel the world, rub elbows with great entertainers, and even exchange autographs with kings—what might you do?

If this book has been about anything, at its core, at its essence, it is about the reality that each and every individual has unlimited possibilities—and certainly the possibility of making themselves important or influential, and doing something of note. *Every* individual.

# Dr. John Brinkley
# ON THE RADIO

The following pages present selected excerpts from a Dr. Brinkley radiobroadcast, circa 1930.

The complete transcript of this broadcast as well as other recordings of John Brinkley broadcasts and a variety of archive materials are in included in the Brinkley Secrets Home Study Course. Information about the Course is online at www.ChipKessler.com

Hi ladies and gentlemen. This is Dr. J.R. Brinkley out of the Brinkley Hospitals in Little Rock, Arkansas speaking to you at this time. And I wonder how many of you men are at this very moment in the condition that one of my patients was in some 2 years ago when he came to me. You know, we get prostate men in all kinds of trouble, far advanced cases as well as mild cases. You know, it's not an easy road doing genitourinary work like we do in the Brinkley Hospitals because you have sick kidneys that are liable to quit on you any minute. You have to be watching your blood pressure and your heart and the kidneys of these patients, and we have to be watching for the secondary anemia that many of them have and general weakness. And because of general weakness they're liable to infection. There are potential death risks in these advanced prostate patients and that's why so many of them die when they're going in for big prostate work.

Now, to give you an idea of the Brinkley work and to let you know that our pathway is not always a bed of roses and we have to handle some of the worst cases that there is, I'm going to read to you a letter from one of my patients, S.A. Carter, 911 Bell Avenue, in Caruthersville, Missouri. This man was carrying 56 ounces of residual urine when he came to us. We advocated blood transfusions to pull him through and now he is a well and a happy man working and enjoying life. But do you realize how much 56 residual ounces are? Thirty-two ounces is one quart and 64 ounces is two quarts and this man was just short 8 ounces of carrying a half a gallon, two quarts of urine, that he couldn't get out of his bladder and his bladder was all distended and it looked as though he had a tumor of some kind in his abdomen, which he did, it was a tumor of water in his bladder that he couldn't empty. And his kidneys were drowned out. And his low-grade anemia and he was practically unconscious and he was a dying man when he was brought into my hospital. A man so sick I couldn't reject him because he would die before he got back home, just like a lot of patients that arrive at my hospital. When they arrive they are so sick that they couldn't even get back home. I really got to work myself and get them well and get them better and send them back home or they're going to die. And this man, Carter out of Caruthersville, Missouri is one of them. He wrote me this letter on the date of February 4, 1939, and he said:

Dear Dr. Brinkley,

I thought I'd write you a letter. Dr. Brinkley,
I don't have words to tell you how much I thank
you for what you've done for me….

And that's one statement that that man could make and mean every
word of it because he can't thank me enough. If it hadn't been that I
gave this man Carter my personal attention, if it had not been that my
associates were on the job, Carter would be dead. He says:

My family doctor told me he couldn't do anything
for me because of my bad prostate and he was
going to send me to Memphis to have it cut out.
But I thought I'd better go to Brinkley Hospital.
I went there on November 28th, 1937. I was so sick
I didn't know whether or not I was going to get
there alive. Well doctor, I got better in three
days and have been getting better all the time. I
eat all I want, sleep like a baby and work every
day. So I think the Brinkley Hospital in Little
Rock, Arkansas, is the place for sick people to
go. I have gained 18 pounds since I came home.

With lots of good wishes to you and family,

Yours truly,
S.A. Carter
911 Bell Avenue
Caruthersville, Missouri

And, as I say, this man was carrying practically one half gallon of residual. He was carrying 56 ounces, lacking 8 ounces of being a half a gallon or two quarts. His kidneys were in serious condition. It was necessary for us to give him blood transfusions. It was necessary for us to give him saline and other solutions, sucrose and tonics and everything else that medical science knows to build a man up and gradually decompress that bladder that was containing 56 ounces of fluid and try to build those kidneys up. And after careful work and conscientious work and hard work, we earned our fee what we charged this man a dozen times, but we were glad to do it and we've paid the lights. And you people want to see a corpse that came back to life and is alive and healthy, I know where you can find one and his name, and that is S. A. Carter, 911 Bell Avenue in Caruthersville, Missouri, because he was just one step outside of an undertaking parlor when he arrived at my hospital. And today he is a healthy man, and as he says, he was so sick that he didn't know whether he was going to reach the Brinkley Hospital alive or not. And when he got into my hospital I thought he was going to be dead before I could do anything for him. And now, he can sleep like a baby, he can work every day, he has gained weight, he can eat all he wants to and anything he wants and what more can a man expect, what more can be done in the way of results for a man than I have done for this man Carter, a dying man when he came to see me. One of the advanced cases any physician, any surgeon would tell you that a man with a prostate so big that it's producing complete obstruction and that the man is carrying 56 ounces of residual urine, that in order to get that man well the doctor that handles the case must know his business. And if you'd like to get well, I don't care if your prostate is as big as a cabbage, I don't care how much residual urine you're carrying or anything about it, if your kidneys are not too far gone so that they respond, if your heart is not too far gone so it will respond, we can pull you through provided we can get you into our hospital before your kidneys are ruined and your heart's ruined. When those kidneys go into uremia and the functioning part of your kidneys quit functioning we are at our end and we can't do anything. The undertaker is the fella that's going to get you. If you want those two books you can have them if you're going to come to see the Brinkley's. If you're going to come to see us or just want the books for the information they contain, send us a dollar and a half and I'll send them. On the other hand, if you're willing to swear on a stack of bibles as high as the moon that you're coming to see us and right away I'll be glad to have a letter from you ordering these books. I'll send you one book first and when you get this first book look it over and study it. When you order the book, be sure and tell me what's the matter with you. If you're a woman, tell me what's the matter with you. If you're a man tell me what's the matter with you. I might write you a personal letter. If I don't write it when I send the book, I'm liable to write it after I get your question blank returned to me, but you better answer all those questions, and answer them honestly and truthfully because I have a way about me that I can usually tell when you're lying a little bit. I don't like you to lie to me. I like you to be honest with me and I want you to answer every question on that question blank, and I want you to answer that last question in which I ask you that if I give you the opportunity to come to the Brinkley Hospital what date is most convenient. And then when I get your blank back if I kind of like you I'll probably send you a date in which I invite you to come and be with us for consultation and examination. If I don't think much of you I probably won't invite you but there's no harm done. You've had the fun of reading the book that didn't cost you anything and filling out the blank. Now you might like to go a little bit further when you get this first book. You might decide that you really do want to be a Brinkley patient, very anxious to be one. In fact so many people never wait to get the second book. A lot of them don't wait to get the first book because they know that these broadcasts are sincere, truthful and honest. They know that these patients are living. They know that both hospitals are filled with patients that have been sent to me by other patients and they know that a man whose hospital stays filled the year round with patients sent to him by other patients is doing a hell of a good job on saving people. But if you decide after you get the first book that you want the second book, the Big Doctor book, then you get that coupon out of that first book and you give me the name of some men that you're personally acquainted with, men that you know that ought to be Brinkley patients, men that you know are physically and financially able to come to see us, and you send those names in to me and in return for your kindness I'll send you the Big Doctor book free. And by that time I'll expect you to be a patient in the Brinkley Hospital.

A letter from my patient G. C. Anderson of Route #3 in Kenton, Tennessee. He says:

Dear Dr. Brinkley,

I was operated on in your hospital on December 15th, 1937, for prostate gland enlargement. I cannot praise you enough for the good work you're doing. I know you are a God-called man. One of my

```
neighbors has just returned from your hospital.
I went with my brother there on January the 31st.
You can read this over the air any way you see
fit. I'd like to tell all the people suffering
with prostate disease to go to the Brinkley
Hospital. I've enjoyed good health.
```

That's G.C. Anderson of Route #3, Kenton, Tennessee, and this man came to me and was operated on in 1937. Then he came to my hospital with one of his brothers. And then one of his neighbors has returned to my hospital. There's three men returned to my hospital. There's three men that were at my hospital. Over there's three men from Tennessee, G.C. Anderson and the brother of Mr. Anderson and one of his neighbors. As I say, former patients keep my hospitals filled with their loved ones and friends and neighbors because of the results that they receive. So what more can you ask for if our patients keep our hospital filled with their friends and their loved ones and neighbors. This man's letter is merely a confirmation of what I've been telling you. My patient comes and he gets well and he maybe brings his father, or the father brings the son, or they bring an uncle or they bring an aunt, or they bring a neighbor. My patients come back, like I told you, one of them came back from Iowa the other day and they brought me four of his neighbors. And sometimes they make a regular automobile load and they come to see us that way.

And let me say to you people who are listening to Dr. Brinkley, if you want to be examined the same day that you arrive at Little Rock the way to do it is to get checked into our hospital not later than 8 o'clock in the morning in the hospital located at the corner of 20th Street and Shore

Avenue. If you get in by 8 o'clock we'll get through with you that day on your examination anyway. And I'm telling you to come now and not delay longer. Delay is dangerous. Delay is risky. And delay is keeping the funeral parlors filled and the undertakers making a fortune. And this is Dr. Brinkley personally speaking to you.

******** Pause **********

Ladies and gentlemen I'm going to read a letter to you from a man that I am going to classify as a real upstanding doctor and American citizen. And this letter comes from Dr. R.C. Thompson of Paris, Arkansas. Dr. Thompson says:

```
Brinkley Hospital
Little Rock, Arkansas

Gentlemen:

Thanks   for   the   invitation   to   attend   your
homecoming. I have just put off coming or writing.
I was operated on for prostate gland disease at
the Brinkley Hospital October 14th, 1937. I was
home the seventh day after the operation…
```

Do you notice that—he was home the seventh day after the operation…

```
…and I have done two men's work every day since.
I had suffered death one thousand times. Went to
St. Louis, Missouri, to the best specialist in St.
```

Louis. I was under the care of four doctors for six days and almost past walking when I returned. I've been thinking of writing Dr. Brinkley a personal letter but I just kept putting it off. I am 20 years younger in every way. I was 76 years of age when operated on and had to be led to the clinic by my son. The reason I have not returned for a recheck is that I felt it was not necessary because it is only a three-hour drive from my home to the Brinkley Hospital in Little Rock. Dr. Brinkley, if you wish, you may announce this over the radio.

R.C. Thompson, M.D.
Paris, Arkansas

Folks I don't know of a stronger endorsement of my work than this letter from this physician, a practicing physician that is well known and beloved by the people in Paris, Arkansas. He is now 76 years of age and had been suffering death, as he said, he had suffered death a thousand times. He went to one of the high priced placed in St. Louis, Missouri. I'm not going to mention the name of it, but it is one of the highly rated places in St. Louis, one of the big places. This doctor went to doctors, friends of his, where he had sent his patients in days gone by. Some of them were shipped back home in a box too. He went to the best specialists in St. Louis on the prostate and four doctors looked after him for six days and when they got through with him good old Dr. Thompson just couldn't walk. And he came to me and he was so sick and so feeble that his son had to lead him to get him around through my hospital to the different examining rooms. He had to be led to the operating room. Had to be helped on the table. He had to be helped off the table. He had to be helped back to his bedroom. But seven days after I operated on Dr. Thompson he was back home in Paris, Arkansas and he didn't have to be helped and he was able to walk. And he says "I'm 20 years younger in every way and the reason I haven't returned for a recheck is I felt it was not necessary, and I'm only a three hour drive from my home to Dr. Brinkley's Hospital in Little Rock." So the man if he was in the least bit of trouble he certainly would drive, take a three-hour drive, to come and see us. So it isn't necessary. He feels 20 years younger, fine in every way. Now doesn't that contrast the Brinkley work to the other work? There's a doctor who goes to the best hospital and the best specialists, four of them work on him for six days, and he can't walk. He has to be led around through my hospital to make the rooms, but he doesn't have to be led out. And in seven days he was back home. He didn't even stay with me for 10 days because it was two days required at that time. My hospital was not in Little Rock at that time. He had to drive two days to get home after he left my hospital. So he stayed with me about five days. Is that anything to be afraid of, that kind of work, and aren't the results glorious? If you have any doubts about it or questions about it consult Dr. R.C. Thompson of Paris, Arkansas. I'm going to tell the doctor right now that I don't expect him to be bothered with answering your letters. He is a busy doctor; he doesn't have time to answer letters, but this is his letter, and Paris, Arkansas is his home. You can go to see him if you want to.

Another letter from Mr. Robert Broadnax of Grand Saline, Texas, says:

```
Dear Dr. Brinkley,

I will write you a few lines to let you know how
I'm getting along. Before I went to your hospital
last November, a year ago, I wasn't able to do my
work but I'm feeling fine now thanks to you.

Robert Broadnax
Grand Saline, Texas
```

Only a few words tell a big story…

<NOTE: RECORDING TRANSCRIPT INTERRUPTED HERE, PORTIONS EXCLUDED. COMPLETE TRANSCRIPT OF THIS AND OTHER RECORDINGS, AUDIO CD'S WITH ACTUAL RECORDINGS AND THER ARCHIVE MATERIALS INCLUDED IN COMPLETE HOME STUDY COURSE—REFER TO WWW.CHIPKESSLER.COM. RESUMING AFTER EXCLUDED PORTION:>

…he was making preparations to come and see me and he died from heart failure and kidney failure before he ever reached me. His widow listens to my broadcasts. And she can truly say along with many other widows he waited too long. His story might have been different, and she agrees it would have been different. She has him to remember by the little radio set I sent him and my talks that come through that radio into her home where there is now saddened by the loss of that husband. And this happens so often and so frequently. There's many widows, thousands of widows, listening to me who write to me and tell me that a husband had planned on coming to see me but he just put it off and didn't get around to it. He was taken suddenly ill. His kidneys quit working. His prostate gland closed off the exit from his bladder. He was taken to the hospital and emergency operation was done. A tube was put into him. He died from the shock. He died from kidney failure. He died from infection. He died from heart failure. He died from hemorrhage. He died from some cause that follows in so many of these cases that wait so long. Is that what you're going to do? Many of you, yes. Many of you, yes. Many of you men are sitting there right now listening to me with your wives and talking about coming to see me after hearing all of this testimony. After hearing that both hospitals are filled with patients sent to me by other patients. After hearing me say come and see for yourselves before you spend a dime. Come into Brinkley Hospitals and talk to all the patients you want to. See what's being done. See what's going on. If you don't like the looks of things you don't have to stay and you don't have to spend a dime. If you do stay you get a fine examination, which costs you $50.00. That examination will tell you what's the matter, and you can either stay and take treatment or pay your $50.00 examining fee and go on back home. I'm inviting you to come now, not to delay longer because so many have died while they were waiting to get started. So come now.

And this is Dr. Brinkley of the Brinkley Hospitals in Little Rock, Arkansas telling you to come to our hospital at the corner of 20th Street and Shore Avenue, Little Rock. Report in by 8 o'clock in the morning and we'll have you examined by the end of that day. And if you come into Little Rock of a night come to the Albert Pike Hotel, a good hotel to stay all night in.

*****************

# RESOURCES

# additional recommended, relevant READING

*Charlatan*—Pope Brock

*There's A Customer Born Every Minute*—Vitale

*Gorgeous George*—Capouya

*Satchel: Life & Times of an American Legend*—Tye

*Secret Life of Houdini*—Kalush/Sloman

*The King of Madison Avenue*—Roman

*How To Get Rich*—Trump

*Profiles of Power & Success*—Landrum

*The Laws of Power*—Greene

*The Untold Story: 20 Years Running The National Enquirer*—Calder

*My Unfinished Business* (Autobiographical Essays)—Kennedy

*Outrageous Advertising*—Glazer

*Uncensored Sales Strategies*—Barrows

**Notes, from Dan Kennedy**: *Charlatan* is the biography of Dr. John Brinkley. Joe Vitale's book, *Customer Born Every Minute*, delves into the advertising, marketing and promotion strategies of P.T. Barnum in similar fashion to our look at John Brinkley's here. *Gorgeous George* tells the inside story of one of the most flamboyant, self-promoting pro wrestlers of wrestling's Golden Age. *Satchel*, about baseball legend, Satchel Page. *Houdini*—this is the definitive biography, with great detail about his self-promotion strategies. *King Of Madison Avenue* is about legendary advertising man David Ogilvy. *How To Get Rich* by and, of course, about Trump. Need we say more? *Profiles of Power and Success* is the first in a series of outstanding, insightful books by Dr. Gene Landrum about the psyche of famous and infamous super-promoters. *Laws of Power* is the seminal work on the principles of power and influence. *The Untold Story* takes you behind the scenes of tabloid journalism and, therefore, the creation and promotion of celebrities. *My Unfinished Business* is the book of mine written for the purpose of creating and strengthening personal relationship with my audience. *Outrageous Advertising* presents a bountiful buffet of contemporary uses of unusual, attention-getting advertising and marketing. *Uncensored Sales Strategies* by former professional madam; the Mayflower Madam, turned sales and 'customer experience' consultant, Sydney Biddle Barrows.

## Online Resources—from the authors

FreeGift.com/JRB

Chip Kessler.com

NoBSBooks.com

DEAR READER,
# YOU'RE
# INVITED
to explore
The Lost Secrets
& Marketing Principles
of John R. Brinkley
in much greater depth and detail,
in an example, exhibit and sample rich
Home Study Course
with print and audio CD resources
assembled by and contributed to by
Chip Kessler and Dan S. Kennedy

# RSVP
www.ChipKessler.com

# an afterword & note from Dan S. Kennedy

Dear Reader,

We hope you enjoyed the book, found some "Gold In The Old", and are intrigued with further, deeper exploration of The 21 Principles.

I have personally profited from my own investigation of John Brinkley's applications of these 21 Principles. As I was working on this book and pouring over the extensive archive of Brinkley advertising and marketing materials, letters, radio broadcasts, scripts, etc. that Chip Kessler and his team collected, with help of family and the Kansas Historical Society, I took several ideas directly to clients and had my work for those clients significantly influenced—and saw impressive results. I can assure you, the remarkable collection of archive materials we've chosen to include (most in their entirety) will similarly inspire you.

Frankly, I can't imagine any true marketer or entrepreneur completing this book and not being eager to get his hands on actual

Brinkley sales tools that demonstrate his 'lost secrets' and principles in action. Of course, the accompanying notes and remarks from Chip and I may prove valuable, too!

To obtain your copy of this complete Home Study Course, please visit: www.ChipKessler.com.

# The Most Incredible
# FREE Gift Ever

## ($573.94 Worth of Pure Money-Making Information)

Dan Kennedy & Bill Glazer are offering an incredible opportunity for you to see WHY <u>Glazer-Kennedy Insider's Circle</u>™ is known as "THE PLACE" where entrepreneurs seeking FAST and Dramatic Growth and greater Control, Independence, and Security come together. Dan & Bill want to give you **$573.94 worth of pure Money-Making Information** including a FREE month as an 'Elite' Gold Member of Glazer-Kennedy's Insider's Circle™. You'll receive a steady stream of MILLIONAIRE Maker Information including:

## * Glazer-Kennedy University: Series of 3 Webinars (Value = $387.00)

### The 10 "BIG Breakthroughs in Business Life *with Dan Kennedy*
- HOW <u>Any</u> Entrepreneur or Sales Professional can Multiply INCOME by 10X
- **HOW to Avoid Once and for All being an *"Advertising Victim"***
- The "*Hidden Goldmine*" in Everyone's Business and HOW to Capitalize on it
- **The BIGGEST MISTAKE most Entrepreneurs make in their Marketing**
- And the <u>BIGGEEE</u>…Getting Customers Seeking You Out.

### The ESSENTIALS to Writing Million Dollar Ads & Sales Letters BOTH
**Online & Offline** *with Marketing & Advertising Coach, Bill Glazer*
- How to INCREASE the Selling Power of <u>All</u> Your Advertising by Learning the <u>13 "Must Have" Direct Response Principles</u>
- **Key Elements that Determine the Success of Your Website**
- HOW to Craft a Headline the Grabs the Reader's Attention
- **How to Create an Irresistible Offer that Melts Away <u>Any</u> Resistance to Buy**
- The <u>Best</u> Ways to Create Urgency and Inspire IMMEDIATE Response
- **"*Insider Strategies*" to INCREASE Response that you <u>Must</u> be using both ONLINE & Offline**

### The ESSENTIALS of Productivity & Implementation for Entrepreneurs *w/*
*Peak Performance Coach Lee Milteer*
- How to Almost INSTANTLY be MORE Effective, Creative, Profitable, and Take MORE Time Off
- **HOW to Master the "Inner Game" of Personal Peak Productivity**
- How to Get MORE Done in Less Time
- **HOW to Get Others to Work On <u>Your</u> Schedule**
- How to Create Clear Goals for SUCCESSFUL Implementation
- And Finally the BIGGEE…How to Stop Talking and Planning Your Dreams and Start Implementing Them into Reality

## * 'Elite' Gold Insider's Circle Membership (One Month Value = $59.97):

- ## An Issue of *The No B.S.*® *Marketing Letter:*

    Each issue is at least 20 pages – usually MORE – Overflowing with **the latest Marketing & MoneyMaking Strategies**. Current members refer to it as <u>a day-long intense seminar in print</u>, arriving by first class mail every month. There are ALWAYS terrific examples of ***"What's-Working-NOW"* Strategies**, timely Marketing news, trends, ongoing teaching of <u>Dan Kennedy's Most IMPORTANT Strategies</u>… and MORE. As soon as it arrives in your mailbox you'll want to find a quiet place, grab a highlighter, and devour every word.

- CD of an **EXCLUSIVE GOLD AUDIO INTERVIEW:**

  These are EXCLUSIVE interviews with <u>successful users of direct response advertising, leading experts and entrepreneurs in direct marketing, and famous business authors and speakers</u>. Use them to turn commuting hours into "POWER Thinking" hours.

  ## * The New Member No B.S.® Income Explosion Guide & CD (Value = $29.97)

  This resource is <u>especially designed for NEW MEMBERS</u> to show them HOW they can join the thousands of Established Members **creating exciting sales and PROFIT growth** in their Business, Practices, or Sales Careers & Greater SUCCESS in their Business lives.

  ### Income Explosion FAST START Tele-Seminar with Dan Kennedy, Bill Glazer, and Lee Milteer (Value = $97.00)

  Attend from the privacy and comfort of your home or office…hear a DYNAMIC discussion <u>of Key Advertising, Marketing, Promotion, Entrepreneurial & Phenomenon strategies</u>, PLUS answers to the most Frequently Asked Questions about these Strategies

## * You'll also get these Exclusive "Members Only" Perks:

- **Special FREE Gold Member CALL-IN TIMES:** Several times a year, Dan & I schedule Gold-Member ONLY Call-In times
- **Gold Member RESTRICTED ACCESS WEBSITE**: Past issues of the *No B.S.® Marketing Letter*, articles, special news, etc.
- **Continually Updated MILLION DOLLAR RESOURCE DIRECTORY** with Contacts and Resources Dan & his clients use.

  To activate your MOST INCREDIBLE FREE GIFT EVER you only pay a one-time charge of $19.95 (or $29.95 for Int'l subscribers) to cover postage (this is for everything). **After your 1-Month FREE test-drive, you will automatically continue at the <u>lowest</u> Gold Member price of $59.97 per month. Should you decide to cancel your membership, you can do so at any time by calling Glazer-Kennedy Insider's Circle™ at 410-825-8600 or faxing a cancellation note to 410-825-3301 (Monday through Friday 9am – 5pm). Remember, your credit card will NOT be charged the low monthly membership fee until the beginning of the next month, which means you will receive 1 full issue to read, test, and** profit from all of the powerful techniques and strategies you get from being an Insider's Circle Gold Member. **And of course, it's impossible for you to lose, because if you don't absolutely LOVE everything you get, you can simply cancel your membership before next month and never get billed a single penny for membership.**

------------------------------------------------------------

**\*EMAIL REQUIRED IN ORDER TO NOTIFY YOU ABOUT THE
GLAZER-KENNEDY UNIVERSITY WEBINARS AND FAST START TELESEMINAR\***

Name _____ Business Name _____

Address _____

City _____ State _____ Postal Code _____ Country _____

e-mail* _____

Phone _____ Fax_____

**Credit Card Instructions to Cover $19.95 ($29.95 Int'l) for Shipping & Handling:**

_____Visa _____MasterCard _____ American Express _____ Discover

Credit Card Number _____ Exp. Date _____

Signature _____ Date _____

**FAX BACK TO 410-825-3301
Or Go To: www.freegiftfrom.com/kessler
Or mail to:  401 Jefferson Ave, Towson, MD 21286**

CPSIA information can be obtained
at www.ICGtesting.com
Printed in the USA
BVHW081641181119
564175BV00004B/192/P

9 780982 379387